CHASING

THE

MAGDALENE

A Personal Journey of Discovery in Provence

and Languedoc.

Cynthia Berresse Ploski

©Copyright 2005
By Cynthia Berresse Ploski

Cover Design by Ralph Williston

_____

First Edition
Copyright © 2005
by

Cynthia Berresse Ploski

_____

Published by Little Eagle Publishing
Lamar, Mo.

Printed and bound in the United States of America.

ISBN 0-9707904-4-9

To the Muse,

Gratefully

For those who wish to find the Holy Grail,

And look towards knights of old, or past

tomorrow,

Be certain that it lies behind the veil

That isolates the heart from inner sorrow.

The journey lies in awakening the soul

To unify with Source, its final goal.

TABLE OF CONTENTS

ACKNOWLEDGEMENTS

A work of this nature can never come to fruition without the pyramid of energy through which the creative force rises. Its foundation is the research made public by the scholars and writers honored in the List of Resources at the end of this manuscript.

Upon this foundation are many layers of building blocks:

—The support and energy of my travelling companions, Karol Teiko, Simon Peter Fuller and Ross Cianci, whose enthusiasm, humor, expertise and fellowship made the journey to France not only enlightening, but fun...

—The love of my husband, Ted Ploski, who gave me space to create, and who always answered "very good" or "yes, dear," when I threw an idea or a chapter at him...

—The feedback of my family, friends and colleagues, who, by reading the manuscript, gave me information that helped me see the story from a point of view outside my own: Melanie Kurtz, Michael Berresse, Penny Ploski, Alissa Berresse, Ellen Berresse; Simon Peter Fuller, Karol Teiko, Mary Carroll Nelson, Betty Rice, Trish Keck, Jerry Stokes, Mitzi Ashcraft, Deborah Hodel and Valaida D'Alessio...

—The spirit of the Holy Feminine, radiating throughout the pyramid... and my publisher, Ralph Williston of Little Eagle Publishing, who provided the gateway for it to enter the world.

Thank you all.

Cynthia Ploski

CE 2005

A NOTE TO THE READER

Since this book is part fiction and part my personal experience, I present it in the spirit of an exploration into new ideas, rather than a book of scholarly research.

The conclusions I draw, which are specifically my own, are not necessarily those of any people featured in the manuscript, and not intended to offend adherents to the orthodoxy of organized religions. In my personal view, however, human beings who are expanding in awareness must seek their own answers to questions that intrigue and puzzle them, rather than accepting, without investigation, traditional dogma.

The tools such seekers use should be education, logic, intuition and personal experience. But there is a lot "out there" to guide the way. Many authorities who are qualified, through education and training, to form expert opinions from the wealth of material presently available, have produced a great deal of information for the benefit of those of us who do not have the same erudite background.

I have relied heavily upon their expertise. You will find these sources of information identified in the List of Resources. I encourage everyone to read the excellent, informative works produced by these investigators into truth.

But in the final analysis, the journey of personal discovery is probably more important than the conclusions of any expert—for there can be many truths, each unique to the point of view of the individual seeker.

With this in mind, I invite you to accompany me on my own journey of discovery, with all its mysteries and its delights, as I sally forth to France, *Chasing the Magdalene*.

INTRODUCTION

Mary Magdalene has been pulling at my sleeve for a long time. It probably began in Sunday School, when I wondered aloud why such a good friend of Jesus should be called a prostitute. I wasn't quite sure what being a prostitute meant, except it was very bad. Teacher flushed, pointedly avoiding an answer to my question. Mary as a sinner made no sense to my child-size brain— or perhaps it was my heart. Immediately a dark veil dropped over the Magdalene's shining face.

During chemotherapy for breast cancer in 1990, I prayed to another Mary, the Virgin Mary, for healing— and was rewarded by an unmistakable energy surge throughout my body, and full recovery. I owe her. She saved my life.

Funny, I thought, *there are two important Marys in Christianity. And there were other Marys in Jesus' inner circle. What's the connection?*

I began considering the possibility that a "Mary" was symbolic of Great Mother—perhaps to our culture what the Goddess was in earlier ages: Feminine Energy personified.

Flash forward…. I am standing in a "crop circle" in England, 1997, the perfect setting for consciousness shaking revelations. Simon Peter Fuller, tour guide, is relating the legend that Mary Magdalene, in the company of a group of Jesus' close friends, fled to the south of France shortly after his crucifixion. Furthermore, they were supposed to have brought the Holy Grail with them. Joseph of Arimathea is said to have carried it on to Glastonbury, England, where he buried it in the famous Glastonbury Well. And Mary Magdalene was reputed to have spent the last 30 years of her life inhabiting a cave in Provence, naked except for her long hair. There, she fasted, taking neither food nor water, but was lifted up to Heaven seven times a day by angels.

What a story! It's not in the history books. Holy Mary must have jumped with joy at the enthusiasm of my reaction.

Would it be possible for me to find the Magdalene alive and well, in the folklore, beliefs, rituals, even the landscape of Provence? The idea was enough to ignite a fire in my heart, carrying me to the South of France the following year. There, I hoped to shine the light of that fire into the flickering shadows of Our Lady of Mystery.

Other voices have been raised in helping unveil this special woman. Researchers of impeccable credibility have delved into her life in the context of those times, revealing her to be the special friend, if not the wife, of Jesus. It is not for me to claim or deny the truth of their research— only to bring my own thoughts, feelings and intuition into what I found awaited me in southern France.

This, then, is the story of how I went looking for the Magdalene, and of the unexpected treasures I discovered along the way.

MONTSÉGUR, View from the Highway

Chapter One

TO FRANCE!

* * * * *

    She wiped a single tear from her weathered face, evidence of love lost. She knew, in her heart, such a great love could never cease to exist; yet she ached for his physical presence, denied to her by his ultimate sacrifice. It was an act that had changed the world. She had let go of all but his memory over these past thirty years. Material possessions meant nothing to her. The cave in which she stood, looking out over the forest below, had become her home and refuge; the angels her companions.

    Leaning against the cool rock wall, she brushed back a cascade of once bright auburn hair, now dull and streaked with silver. It hung loosely below her waist, as it had long ago in the Temple of Isis, before her marriage. Falling in tangles across her worn garment, it barely hid her nakedness— a garment as tattered as her reputation in their beloved homeland. Harlot! they had called her, those Sadducees. Satan incarnate!

    Had the priestess really fallen so low? She, whose long copper tresses had once wiped dry the feet of her beloved? She, who had anointed him with precious oil?

    Not so, not here in Gaul. She smiled now, at the thought of multitudes flocking to hear her speak the Love he brought to all mankind. Their faces had glowed with light her words kindled within their hearts.

1

They adored her in this foreign land.

Too humble to accept their total adulation, and seeking to elevate her spirit to the level of his own, she had left her grown children, her friends and the crowded towns to find solitude in this cavern. So like the womb of Mother Earth, yet high on the face of a rocky mountain!

But even in this self-imposed isolation, she could not leave the memories behind. They were part of her. They trailed along in her wake, as she slowly moved deeper into the soft darkness of her refuge.

Sinking down upon a bed of furs, she surrendered to those persistent memories, reliving them once again.

* * * * *

Somewhere over the mid-Atlantic my heartbeat slows and blood pressure returns to normal. The rear end of my pants, which is beginning to suffer seriously from confinement in the cramped seats of our huge jet airplane, calls for attention

"Flex them, one side at a time," Karol whispers below the roar of the craft's engines. I notice she is bobbing almost imperceptibly up and down in the seat beside me.

"You're kidding." She just smiled. I tried it. It works. But the thought of the two of us, surrounded by a swell of unaware humanity, surreptitiously flexing our backsides, drove us into giggles. Laughter broke the tension of preparing for our exciting and unusual trip.

You understand, two years as college roommates in the 1950's spawned intimacy of mind and similarity of purpose. Karol's and my interim decades had followed similar paths: marriage, four children each, divorce, remarriage, careers in the arts— she, an opera singer, and I, a visual artist and writer. Resuming our friendship during the past ten years found us comfortably and compatibly running off to adventures in New

England and Greece. "Two old Broads Abroad," we laughingly called ourselves. Now we were on our way to Provence and Languedoc in the South of France—to do *what?* To try to find Mary Magdalene.

This journey had been more than a year in planning, ever since Simon Peter Fuller, standing in the middle of a magnificent crop formation called the "Torus" in England had told me the legend of Mary Magdalene's coming to France. We were on a tour of Sacred Sites in connection with an exhibition and meeting of my art group, the Society of Layerists in Multi Media, in Marlborough. Crop formations regularly appear in the area known as the Wessex Triangle, near Stonehenge, Avebury and Glastonbury. And this magnificent one had conveniently materialized virtually (and literally) underfoot.

"There is historical evidence," Simon Peter, who was one of our affable tour guides, confided to me and anyone within earshot, "that shortly after Jesus' crucifixion, Mary Magdalene and others brought the Holy Grail to France, and Joseph of Arimathea carried it here to England. It is said to have been buried in the well at Glastonbury."

"Really?" I was intrigued, never before having heard this bit of history.

"The story is," Peter continued, "that a boatload of Saints, all close friends of Jesus, were shipwrecked near Marseilles, close to the town of Les Saintes-Maries-de-la-Mer. They are supposed to have built a church there and to have remained in Provence the rest of their lives."

"No kidding?" I pressed Peter for more, toying with a bent ear of bearded wheat I had just picked off the ground. Bathed in warm English sunshine, my fellow artists were exploring the immense, intricate formation around us; meditating, photographing, sketching, dowsing its energies. *Earth energies*, it seemed to me, *feminine energies.*

Peter snapped my attention back to his story.

"There is a Basilica in the town of Maximim-la-Sainte-

3

Baume where you can see Mary Magdalene's skull."

"Her *skull?* You're quite serious!" I dropped the strand. It joined its siblings on the beautifully interwoven Torus formation floor, satiny gold. I looked up at Peter, fully focused now. My eyes must have blazed fascinated skepticism.

"Check your tour books," he smiled broadly, noting my reaction. "I think Saint Martha's bones are somewhere near there as well."

"Peter, this is so amazing! After this tour ends I am joining a friend from California in Germany. The two of us are taking a train down the Rhône Valley to Provence. We'll be making the journey of the Holy Grail in reverse!"

"I wish I could go with you," Peter sighed, "but I have other tours lined up. Why don't we plan a trip there next year, in the Fall, when my tours have ended for the season? I am working on setting up tours for the following year, that follow the Magdalene and the Heresies that sprang up after and around her—the Grail, Cathars, Knights Templar and Black Madonnas."

"Wouldn't that be nice?" I replied excitedly, caught in the magical moment. Yet after cold reality flashed a warning, I demurred. Restrictive thoughts of finances, responsibilities and like limitations barged in, crowding out the magic. "Well anyway, Peter, let's do keep in touch by e-mail. You never can tell, perhaps it will work out."

I should not have sold the Magdalene short, but at that time I did not realize how much she wanted us to seek her. Little did I know....

The rest of my journey that summer had been planned too long in advance to change itinerary. Our precious few days in Provence nevertheless turned up literature that referred to Mary Magdalene's arrival, along with Saints Mary Jacoba, Mary Helena, Sarah, Mary Magdalene's "sister" Martha and "brother" Lazarus, preaching the new religion of Jesus' words. Could the stories be true after all? Leaving Provence was like tasting the first bite of a scrumptious ice cream sundae and having the rest snatched away,

4

spoon in mid air. But it did intensify my desire to plunge back into that hot fudge —and this time, finish the bowl.

Months passed. Peter, who still wanted to connect in Provence, stayed in touch. I began researching what others had written about Jesus and his culture. A clearer picture of those times emerged.

For example, did you ever, like me, wonder why there are so many "Marys" in the New Testament? Apparently, "Mary" (after Miriam, the sister of Moses) was a title, not a name, given to certain women among the Essenes, a sect of ascetic Jews living at Qumran, near Jerusalem. These "Marys" are believed to have functioned as priestesses, leaders of liturgy among females. In translation upon translation, "Mary" eventually became thought of as Mary, a proper name.

In losing the understanding of the name's source, perception of the woman's identity and role in society also disappears.

Then, along about Christmastime, Karol telephoned.

"Well, Cinnie, where are we going next?"

"Karol, I have this crazy idea about going to the south of France."

"Done!" she exclaimed into the telephone. That sealed it.

So here we were, early October 1998, actually on the airplane, zooming through space, moving toward sunrise across the Atlantic. Two senior citizens periodically bobbing up and down to relieve our aching backsides. Pretty unlikely sleuths to unravel history.

I'm so glad Mary Magdalene has a sense of humor.

5

THE FOUR ADVENTURERS:
Ross, Karol, Peter and Cynthia

Chapter Two

LADIES AND GENTLEMEN, A SCENARIO

* * * * *

The light, that glorious light of sunset, faded outside her cave, gently drawing the curtain of darkness across its opening as she pulled the furs of her bedding around herself.

Something wonderful was going to happen; she knew it in every cell of her body. Something was going to alter her peaceful solitude—and it would be good. The thrill of secret anticipation would not leave her in peace.

At long last, she closed her eyes, sinking into sleep.

A happy dream drifted into her slumber. It felt less a remembrance than a reenactment. She seemed to be, once again, in the bedroom of the little home they shared near Qumran, when he was not on duty in the monastery. Moonlight was spilling through the window and across the floor, climbing up the side of their bed to wash his face in its pale glow. She had just come back from satisfying the hunger of their firstborn, Tamar, in the other room. Drawing the doorway's curtain softly behind her, she moved to approach her husband..

How beautifully his long eyelashes curled across his cheek! Her heart nearly stopped, feeling a rush of supreme ecstasy, exalted in the realization he was her husband at last, truly and forever. The trial marriage over, the final vows pronounced, she was his wife in the eyes of the Law, and of God. Nothing could separate them now!

Quietly easing herself down beside him, she felt his body shift as he stirred.

"Sleep now, my precious," she whispered, "the babe is full of milk and at peace." He made a soft sound, turning towards her. She felt the weight of his protective arm across her shoulders, holding her close. Outside the window, the scent of night-blooming flowers flowed into the room on rivers of moonbeams, and they slept.

Now, waking, she opened her eyes to cold reality. For the first time she felt dissatisfaction with her retreat from the world. Being close to him again in dreams had awakened every sensitivity. She missed his presence keenly—as keenly as those first days after the mockery they called his crucifixion.

But this beautiful dream—ah, it gladdened her heart with the same joy she felt when he emerged alive from that cold tomb!

The woman shivered, drawing her ragged garment close around her shoulders. She knew it was only a dream, but—how strange!—she could still clearly smell the flowers of the night.

* * * * *

Our giant airborne fly droned on...and on...into the night. Drinks and dinner over, bored with actors shooting silently at each other and blowing up buildings on the overhead TV screens, I try to catch some sleep. Eyes closed against the light and pillow stuffed under my ear, I try. Sliding down in the seat, pillow under chin, I try. Twisting to the left, elbows on the arm of the seat, I try. Twisting to the right, no better. Finally I give up and simply close my eyes, creating a personal movie on the inside of my eyelids.

Scene one of my scenario opens in a small house on the outskirts of Jerusalem. Jesus has recently been crucified. The room is crowded with women wearing brown cloaks. Mary Magdalene's is black. I wonder why hers is a different color.

The Magdalene moves toward a small boy and older girl,

8

and I see that she is pregnant. Obviously the children's mother, she gestures them authoritatively towards a sweet faced old woman sitting in a corner, sewing garments.

"Yeshua, Tamar, go sit by your grandmother. You can help her, and not be under our feet all the time." She is not really angry with them, just busy.

That old woman must be— wait now— another Mary, mother of Jesus. Yes! That is who she is. The children run to her, calling "Grandmother." She gathers them into her arms, hugging warmly, returning their smiles with a toothless grin of her own. Then she hands them pieces of fabric to fold into neat piles. They cheerfully obey her orders.

The younger women appear to be bustling about, preparing for a journey. One with light brown hair is bundling up provisions. "Sister Martha," calls Mary Magdalene, "Sarah has more matzoth in the kitchen for you to wrap." The brown haired woman nods, moving to the kitchen where a beautiful, dark skinned woman wearing golden earrings hands her bundles of flat, round unleavened bread.

"Mary Helena and Mary Jacoba," directs the Magdalene, who is definitely in charge, "Please go to the house of Brother Lazarus and tell him we are almost ready. But be sure to cover your faces and stay in the shadows lest the Roman troops recognize you. Hurry back before dusk! It is dangerous for any of us to be out there." Nodding, the two women draw cloaks over their heads and furtively leave the house.

Scene two: The women have returned and everyone is sitting around the table about to share an evening meal, when a harsh knock shakes the door. Two men burst in without waiting for it to be opened.

"Where is your Master?" cries the first one; burly, surly, of martial demeanor. He could have been a soldier, if he had not been dressed like an upstanding Roman citizen. "We heard he has appeared to you."

Mary Magdalene rises as gracefully as her condition

permits, drawing her black cloak around the unborn child as if to protect it. Her glorious red hair falls loosely over its folds.

"He has not been with us since that time in the Upper Room, Saul," she replies softly, brushing a lock aside. "Please join us, Peter too." She invites the men, glancing past Saul to Peter; gesturing to her place at the table. Peter, clearly nervous, averts his eyes, anxiously fingering the short dagger shoved into his belt.

"Then who has begotten that bastard in your womb, pray tell?" Saul spits on the floor in frustration. He sweeps a circle with his arm, beckoning Peter to follow him subserviently out of the door.

"Harlot! Now I see for certain you have seduced the man they call the son of God!" Saul shouts as they stride through the damaged door. Peter shuffles out in his wake, still refusing to look at her, concerned as much for his own safety as for theirs.

Pandemonium erupts among the women. The room shakes with their jostling. The whole house seems to be lurching and bumping. A loud male voice is heard proclaiming, Godlike, from somewhere far above:

"WE ARE FLYING THROUGH SOME TURBULENCE, LADIES AND GENTLEMEN. PLEASE FASTEN YOUR SEAT BELTS."

Zut, alors! Just when things were getting exciting!

Our airplane bucks and thumps, a wild horse resisting the saddle. Once quiet returns, I unbuckle my seat belt, settling back into reverie. Now I become the reviewer critiquing my own movie.

Do you think people will be shocked at Mary's being pregnant? I ask myself.

Only those with closed minds, another part of my brain responds.

There is good reason to believe Mary Magdalene and Jesus were married and had children, the logical half continues, making its point emphatically in my head.

The first time I encountered this theory was when I read

10

the seminal book *Holy Blood, Holy Grail,* by Michael Baigent, Richard Leigh and Henry Lincoln, back in 1983. It was a shocker at the time, proposing that Jesus had progeny with Mary Magdalene, and it was their bloodline which constituted the real Holy Grail.

Sang Réal in French, means *Royal Blood.* San-greal, if you choose to pronounce it that way. English speaking people mispronouncing and mistranslating the first syllable as *Saint* and the second as *Grail* transformed it into *Holy Grail.* Without a rigid religious background, I had no problem considering the possibility of a bloodline descending from the pair. Why not? Did it make Jesus any less inspiring?

Another woman, devout Roman Catholic and Biblical scholar, read this same book. Horrified, she decided to do her own research, and came up with similar conclusions. Margaret Starbird then presented her new awareness to the world in a movingly beautiful book, *The Woman with the Alabaster Jar.* When I read her story, I was further convinced there was truth to be found in the legends.

Hmmm, I thought, returning to my scenario, *I should have had Peter show more fear. Saul was persecuting all the associates of Jesus, and he had heard rumors of the Master's reappearance.*

Peter hated the Magdalene. Do you think I should have had him throw a stone at her?

And what of Saul? We know him as Paul. Perhaps I made him a little too tough and rough. Who knows what he really looked like? Maybe tall and handsome, possibly a con man, smooth and polite. Yes, definitely a con man.

The thought of Paul brought me back to present awareness. Paul molded the Roman Catholic Church according to his own interpretation of what Jesus taught. He didn't like women, either, even more than Peter (who actually had a wife.) That dislike of women is pretty evident, seems to me, since he made the church a male domain—except for one perfect and chaste token female,

11

the Virgin Mary.

Everybody loves a mother.

No doubt Jesus loved her too, but he would have been more respectful of women in general, and supportive of his female friends in particular.

And what about this Jesus? They called him Yeshua. Who actually was this man? What was he really like?

In 1947, the Dead Sea scrolls were found near Qumran. They were books of sacred Hebrew literature hidden in the 4th century AD. Recent researchers, noting similarities between earliest Christianity and accounts in the Dead Sea Scrolls, speculate that Jesus emerged from the Essene group of Jews who lived in that area.

He was called a Nazarene, the common belief being he came from the town of Nazareth. Nazareth, however, did not exist at the time Jesus was born. Nazarenes of that epoch were Essenes who practiced very high spiritual ideals. I believe Jesus was probably one of them. Women among the Essenes were often honored as healers and spiritual leaders.

With a little *humph* I returned to my imaginary film set, trying to mentally refigure Saul's entrance into the house of women. But I couldn't seem to rewrite the script. Soon my mind surrendered, settling into a fitful doze, while the huge bird in which we passengers were flying to Paris, very like a multitude of Jonahs in the belly of the whale, carried us forward through the ridiculously short night.

Much too soon, flight attendants came striding through the passenger cabin, pulling up window shades, cheerily announcing that morning had indeed arrived, and we were only an hour out of Paris. Orange juice, croissants and coffee brought us back to the real world, ready to land in a driving rainstorm, collect our baggage and transfer to the plane for Marseilles.

Charles deGaulle airport has to be the most confusing terminal in the world. Even if you speak French. And mine was either really rusty or I was really tired. Probably both. Collecting baggage and going through customs was easy— we just followed the crowd. But being on our own to find "Halle D" in the 45 minutes allowed for transfer proved a virtually insurmountable task for us.

"S'il vous plâit, monsieur, où est Halle D?"

"Là bas, madame." This, accompanied by a vague wave of the arm. So we hauled our suitcases in the direction the busy official indicated. No sign of Halle D. No hope but to try the question again, this time with a lady in uniform. A torrent of incomprehensible but sympathetic words cascading over our heads, we tried to follow her gestures. Out of the building, into another, down the stairs, up the escalator. We finally arrived breathlessly at Halle D with one minute, one blessed minute, to spare.

At last, squeezed into two adjoining seats, Karol and I relaxed, congratulating each other. We were going to get to Provence after all! But looking out the window as we rose through the pelting dawn to our cruising altitude, nothing but clouds could be seen below. Socked in. All the way to Marseilles. *Quel dommage!*

As we approached our destination, however, a miracle occurred. We landed in a great burst of early morning sunshine, the very same light which captured 19th century Impressionist painters, holding them enraptured prisoners in that magical countryside.

And we, alighting with greatest joy to greet it, delighted in the glory too.

It was a good omen.

13

LES SAINTES-MARIES-DE-LA-MER:
Our Lady of the Unknown Universe

Chapter Three

THE-HOLY-MARYS-OF-THE-SEA

* * * * *

Still shivering, wide awake now from that happy dream, she drew her warm deerskin blanket up against the night's cold. Was it the air, or was this chill a memory of the fear that had driven them from their homeland after he had been released from the tomb? Fear for her life, for herself and the others Yeshua had loved, fear for her children and the one that had yet to be born?

It was now so long past! Oddly, though, tonight it felt like all this had happened only a moment ago. The memories came closer, sharp and clear.

Once again she trembled at the hate in Peter's voice as he begged to know what Yeshua told her in private. Peter had been so jealous when the Master talked to her alone, kissed her on the mouth with lingering caresses, drew her aside to hold her close! Did Peter not realize she had anointed him, that he was her husband?

"Women should not be allowed to live!" he spat, as if she were an ant to be crushed beneath his sandal.

She had known they must flee in secrecy, and quickly, lest so many who hated them destroy the truth she carried in her heart and in her womb. She had a friend in the palace who honored her noble birth. He would help her. They could sail to Gaul, that beautiful land of flowers and rare birds, black bulls and white horses, light and peace.

Remembering the moment they set sail, dark of night, in fearful silence, she felt vast relief flooding her heart. They

15

had arrived safely. All had turned out well.

She rose from her bed, and drawing the furs tighter around her thin body, walked slowly to the cave's entrance, feeling her way along its familiar walls. In the black velvet heavens outside, stars glittered brightly, full of beauty, full of hope. It was a night just like this that they had left their homeland, Palestine!

That memory returned, now even more sharply drawn than her dream of Yeshua. She recalled the terror this secret voyage had held for the little boat full of passengers escaping from chaotic Jerusalem.

How were they to have known a terrible storm awaited them? Once again she heard the screaming wind, the crashing waves. Her body felt anew the shock of splintering mast, the dangerous flailing of torn and tattered sails a hand's width from their heads. Once again the wails of her terrified children echoed in her ears as they clung, lashed together, to the stump of the mast, until wind and waves finally abated.

Dawn, that precious morning, had revealed a narrow strip of land far in the distance. It seemed to be an island close by the mouth of a huge river. Weak and exhausted, everyone sank to their knees on the battered blue boat, praising God, singing.

The current was carrying them closer and closer! Joyfully, the passengers embraced each other, while a huge pink bird circled the wreck, leading them to safety. When they finally washed ashore, lying exhausted on the sand, the pink bird and its mate stood guard, like angels.

Yes, she remembered, staring at the stars; but why on this night, of all nights, does it seem to have happened only yesterday?

Hope and anticipation spread through her frail form, stirring new energy into its cells.

* * * * *

16

It is not necessary, driving through Provence, to imagine Van Gogh's paintings hanging in museums. There were real life ones, around us, everywhere.

"Look to your left, Karol," I pointed. She glanced out the driver's window to see a small drawbridge spanning a canal. "I'm certain that's the one we have seen in books."

"You're right," she marveled, it could be the very same bridge." It was—or I believe it was—for later I learned that the famous drawbridge had indeed been restored and still spans the Arles Canal. That's where we were driving, along the A-54 AutoRoute toward Arles. And there was that cute little bridge, minus the horse and carriage, of course.

Sleep deprivation heightened the surreality of rolling through a sunny Impressionist morning. *Impossible! 12 hours earlier we were in Newark Airport! Another continent, another day. Wow.*

"Did you say something?" Karol, was adjusting the rear view mirror.

"No, I was just thinking how unreal this all seems."

"You bet. But we both need to stay in present time. You're the navigator, remember? We drew straws. You have the map, I have the wheel. We want to get to Les Saintes-Maries-de-la-Mer today."

The Holy-Marys-of-the-Sea. What a curious name. Our guidebook confirmed what Peter had told us, that a boatload of people, including Mary Magdalene, her "sister"(much like "nun") Martha and "brother" (as in monk) Lazarus, Mary Jacoba, Mary Helena, and an Egyptian slave named Sarah were shipwrecked here shortly after Jesus was crucified. I wondered who these people really were. Did they actually come to the shores of Les Saintes-Maries-de-la-Mer? Or is it just a story, folklore, myth; or perhaps simply a tourist trap?

Following Karol's reasonable advice, I let go of the imaginings, content to stay in the moment. It was easy to take pleasure in the bliss of paintings revealing themselves along the roadside. Here a Cézanne cottage, there a Matisse landscape. Autumn had brightened the trees and vineyards to Van Gogh hues, while glorious early morning light brought every picture into glowing, sharp detail.

Karol had adapted well to driving the car we rented at the airport. We had wheeled our bulky, overcrowded luggage cart across the parking lot and into, yes *into* the tiny, crowded, temporary rental office building, much to the amusement of a number of businessmen waiting in line. But the lady behind the counter, nonplussed, sped us smoothly through the paperwork.

This was the first of many times I initiated an inquiry in French, to which someone responded in fluent English.

"English, not *American*," insists Peter Fuller, laughing. He's English, we're American. He speaks English; we speak American. He's right. Time has brought many differences to our languages.

But I digress. Madame-of-the-rental-cars put all our papers in order and sent us to a little green Renault, parked with her nose six inches away from a wall. Karol, taking the first turn, slid into the driver's seat, started up the engine and gleefully announced, "We're off!"

No, we were *not* off. We were nudging forward, threatening the wall.

"Gosh, I thought I had it in reverse," she muttered. Pushing down on the gearshift, shoving it from neutral into gear, we moved, again.

Forward.

"Let me try," I offered. Neither of us had driven a stick shift in a long time, but we thought we would remember. Just like riding a bicycle, right?

Wrong. I tried in vain. I know that in most cars you have to push the floor mounted gearshift down to move into reverse. Maybe in this car you have to pull *up?* I yank the knob hard— same result as before. The little green Renault, with a mind of its own, moves only one direction, threatening the integrity of that darkly stoic wall. Karol was ready for expert advice.

"Why don't you go back to the office and ask someone how to get this darn thing in reverse?" she suggests logically. Madam-of-the-Rental-Cars chuckles good naturedly, summoning a young man standing by the door. *"Allez-vous aider ces femmes, s'il vous plaît,"* she requests of the lad, nodding in the direction of the parking lot.

"Sure. OK." Big smile, as he trots to the car, leaving me hustling behind, in his bubbling energy wake. I catch up to him at the Renault.

"You see? You see? Like *zees!*" He demonstrates, pulling upwards on an inconspicuous ring located invisibly just *below* the gearshift knob, smoothly shifting into reverse. The little green car, like a well-trained puppy, obediently edges backwards.

"Merci beaucoup," We thank him profusely, and profoundly humbly.

"Sure. OK." Big smile.

It's all in knowing how.

So at last we found ourselves on the AutoRoute, following the map north and west, turning south at Arles and heading into the Camargue towards Les Saintes-Maries-de-la-Mer.

It was at a beach bordering the Camargue, that swampy coastal plain, where the boatful of Marys was supposed to have landed, back around A.D. 40. I wondered how it had looked at the time.

Vineyards blurred into rice paddies as we entered the Camargue region. Cézanne houses transformed into the thatched roof *Mas*, farmhouses where the *gardiens*, French equivalent of American cowboys, live. Stolid, white, immovable, each Mas presents a windowless back wall to the frequent cold Mistral winds roaring down the Rhône Valley to the Mediterranean Sea. Tilted upon each windswept brown thatched roof, a small cross bears witness that God fearing folk dwell within. From time to time we caught glimpses of the barren, sandy seashore, pink flamingos strutting upon the strand.

19

White horses seemed to be everywhere. Always white. Strong horses. Sturdy as the Mas themselves in this timeless landscape.

"Why do you suppose they are all white?" Karol wondered out loud. I had no answer.

There were cows, too— no, bulls, lots of them. And they were all black.

Maybe this really is a magical land.

Eventually, signs indicated we were getting close to Les Saintes-Maries-de-la-Mer. Our *auberge* was north of the town itself, so we put off visiting it, in favor of settling down to enjoy an absolutely essential rest. We were the only guests. The kitchen was closed. The season had ended just the previous day and everyone was on vacation, leaving a lovely young woman, who knew very little about running a business, in charge.

Too tired to care about food, we flung ourselves upon twin beds in our room, which fronted a beautiful, unused swimming pool, and slept for a deep, dreamless hour.

Refreshed by the nap, we drove into the cheerful, holidayish, boutique-filled, internationally-salted, gypsy-peppered Les Saintes-Maries-de-la-Mer. A cobweb of narrow streets leading from the seaside esplanade gathered in tight circles around the central fortress of a huge, solid church.

Karol and I wasted no time in the boutiques. Straight to the church we strode. So close at last to our treasure! Shopping, though tempting—oh yes—could wait!

Entering by a side door, we found ourselves in a vast space, empty except for rows of wooden pews. To our left, in the usual location, stood a simple altar. Very high in a wall above it, a large niche held two painted metal coffins. Below the altar, stairs led down to a crypt. The glow of many candles in that subterranean crypt flowed up through the stairway into the dimly lit church, but we were too far back to see what was inside that deep, soft light.

We turned towards the wall immediately to our left.

20

There they were! Within a flower laden recess, statues of two beautiful ladies stood calmly in a little blue boat. Dark haired Saint Mary held a chalice in her left hand, the right raised in blessing. Red haired Saint Mary stood on her left, hands clasped in prayer. The two women, standing forever in their impossibly tiny blue boat, gazed serenely out over the empty church.

Riveted to the spot by their presence, awe flooded the hearts of these two latter day pilgrims who had crossed an ocean in less than a day to visit them. A miracle in itself.

We had found the Saintes-Maries. But there were only two of them! Which ones? St. Mary Helena and St. Mary Jacoba, said the guidebook.

What happened to the others?

And where was Mary Magdalene?

And what is the chalice that one is holding, if not the Holy Grail?

21

LES-SAINTES-MARIES-DE-LA-MER:
The Two Saints Mary of the Sea

Chapter Four

WHO WAS MARY MAGDALENE ANYWAY?

* * * * *

Why was it she felt so close to him this particular night? Memories continued to spill unbidden into her mind. She could almost see the radiance of his countenance, that time he surprised her at the door of his tomb. Why, as she reached to touch him, that morning, had he sent her away?

"Our time will come," he had said, "I must be about my mission. I have chosen you above the rest to tell the others I have risen from the dead."

Her joyous heart had broken at his withdrawal, but she knew him well. "When shall we be together again?" she had pled, tears of joy and sorrow blending, her hands clasped in supplication, eyes downcast.

"We shall never really be apart," he answered softly. "You will see. But there is much to do before I return. Carry on my work. The people need our love."

Sensing him so close to her now, she turned her back away from the night sky, once more moving carefully along the wall to her bed.

Yes, she thought, I have carried on your work, but now I am tired and old. Our precious children have grown and left me. My strength has deserted me as well. I feel as weak as that terrible day I stood with your dear mother and my sisters Jacoba and Helena at the foot of the cross, helplessly watching your dreadful agony. Only memories of

the happy days we were together in Migdol and Bethany and
Jerusalem sustain me.

I no longer have need for copious food or drink. It
seems I grow lighter in body day after day. Soon, perhaps, I
shall be reunited with you in the eternal joy of Heaven.

But in her heart new life beat restlessly stronger.

* * * * *

Mary Magdalene was not in Les Saintes-Maries-de-la-Mer after all. We would have to keep on chasing her. Was she a real person or a symbol? Wife or concubine? Was she priestess or prostitute?

Just who was Mary Magdalene anyway?

One thing is for sure, the Magdalene was never a prostitute. She was Mary of Magdala according to the Gospels. Her name was always written in that same respectful way and survived (which most women's names did not) the editing processes of the New Testament. Always the same name, Mary-of (from)-Magdala. Although very little is actually said about her in the Gospels, she plays a critical role. Mary stood with Jesus' mother watching the Crucifixion. It was to Mary of Magdala that Jesus first revealed himself after his resurrection. It was she who was sent to tell the other apostles the good news. That is, if you don't listen to Paul, who left her out of that scene completely.

Paul may have been simply trying to bolster his own authority by including himself with those who had seen the risen Christ; but it is true he did omit Mary's name from that episode. He left out most other women as well. Why? It seems clear Paul wanted to steer the fledgling church into his own belief system; which, having certain pivotal differences from Jesus' teachings, was to eventually result in a male hierarchy.

I pondered, standing before the two Marys in the boat, why different interpreters of Scripture throughout the centuries have seen Mary Magdalene as one, or a combination of three separate women— Mary of Magdala, Mary of Bethany, and a

24

nameless sinner. Each of them anointed the Master.

Who were these women?

Bethany was a town in Judea near Jerusalem. Jesus and his disciples spent a week there just before his triumphant entrance into Jerusalem as King of the Jews. It was in Jerusalem, so soon afterwards, that he was betrayed and crucified. This Mary of Bethany was said to have washed Jesus' feet, wiped them with her hair and anointed him with expensive oil from an alabaster jar. Mary of Bethany was also the one who sat at Jesus' feet while her "sister" (fellow believer) Martha did household work for the comfort of their guests. And Jesus said that was the better way to live, with the emphasis on spiritual matters rather than mundane daily chores.

I smiled to myself with that thought. I never did like household chores.

Another woman thought to be Mary Magdalene was the repentant sinner who burst into a house where Jesus was dining with Pharisees. She barged in weeping, proceeding to wash his feet with her tears, dry them with her long hair and anoint them with oil.

The third is Mary of Magdala. This Mary was an important and influential woman, a minister among other women, healer, well respected and of great dignity. She too was said to have anointed Jesus, and in the Apocryphal literature she was portrayed as his favorite among the apostles; his intimate companion.

Many Biblical scholars have integrated these three women into one Mary of Magdala. The debate still rages between people of opposing opinions. My personal belief is all three women are Mary Magdalene, seen by Gospel writers in various aspects and events.

The one who was known as Mary of Magdala was born, there seems no dispute, in the town of Migdol, a prosperous fishing community on the shores of the Sea of Galilee, 6 kilometers northwest of the town of Tiberius.

According to Chevalier Laurence Gardner (*Bloodline of the Holy Grail*) Mary Magdalene's father was the Chief Priest who officiated at the great marble synagogue at Capernaum. She was said to have been "raised" (initiated) in A.D. 17 at age 14. This would place her birth in 3 B.C. Jesus was most probably born in 7 B.C.

Mary's mother, a woman named Eucharia, was related to the Royal (Hasmonaean) House of Israel, not the Royal (Davidic) House of Judah, to which Jesus belonged. Mary, being of the Hasmonaean kingly line, entered the world on a very high level of social status.

The Gnostic belief system, which coexisted with Christianity during the first century, gave Mary great respect. *Pistis Sophia* is a Gnostic document which tells the story of the resurrected Savior, who returns to spend twelve years teaching his disciples before his final ascension. Mary Magdalene is one of the holy women, with Mary Salome, and Mary the mother of Jesus, among the disciples. It is the Magdalene who is the chief questioner, seen as inheritor of the Light, the incarnation of Wisdom (Sophia) and feminine counterpart of Christ. As such, she symbolizes the Holy Spirit.

Not bad for a "prostitute."

A Roman Catholic nun and Biblical scholar, Mary Thompson, S.S.M.N., writes (*Mary of Magdala, Apostle and Leader*) that in no place within the canonical gospels is that association made. She states that Mary is clearly shown as a leader in the apocryphal gospels.

So how did she become known as a prostitute? Amazingly, by the late 6th Century Mary Magdalene had been completely reconstructed from an apostle into a repentant sinner.

Although Jesus flaunted the cultural mores of his day by ministering and preaching to women, even including them in his entourage, his successors reflected more customary attitudes. Existing at the bottom of Hebrew social strata, women were seen as "unclean" because they menstruated. By many, they were not even considered to have souls.

In the early Church, Paul was forced to recognize the efforts of certain women who formed pockets of worship in their homes, supporting his ministry. But within his circle, he did not elevate any of them to participation in the priesthood or any other ecclesiastical functions.

Susan Haskins tells us in *Mary Magdalen, Myth and Metaphor,* that the African church Father Tertullian proclaimed, near the end of the second century, that women are not permitted to speak in the church, nor allowed to teach, baptize or offer the Eucharist. Further, women are not allowed to share in any masculine function, let alone the office of priest.

The main issue seems to have been one of power. In the Essene tradition, from which Jesus probably emerged, women could hold high offices. Such a person was Mary Magdalene.

There were women, in the days of Paul's ministry, who did wear the scarlet robes of bishops, or the black robes (as did the Magdalene) of Priestesses of Isis. Paul did not care for women wearing those vestments; but had to allow them, since those influential women were important in helping spread and support his doctrine. However, he never created ecclesiastical offices for women. He simply allowed those that already existed among groups of converts to his cause to continue. In this century we would say he "grandfathered them in."

Consider the colors: Red is a symbol of power. Red robes are worn by (male) bishops even today.

As an artist, I know that black is also powerful, since black absorbs all colors of the spectrum contained within light. One step in the process of disempowering women occurred when Rome, in 1659, issued a decree proclaiming that all images of the Virgin Mary (the only woman allowed veneration in the Roman Catholic Church) must be clad in blue and white. Calm colors. Quiet colors. Non threatening colors. Yes, Jesus was a rebel. He believed in equality of male and female, but unfortunately his apostolic successors reverted to the prevailing cultural attitudes of their time— which was "men, yes; women, no."

Ancient Goddess cosmology, passed down through the ages, in which Cybele, Diana, Demeter, Juno, Isis, and other female deities coexisted with, and sometimes dominated, their male counterparts, had been discarded earlier when the Hebrew Religion established itself under one (male) God. Female power, the power of creation, was necessarily made subservient as a result. Subjugation of women can only be maintained through control by a male authority system.

Therefore, in the context of the newly formed Christian religion, descending directly from Judaic tradition, it became essential to discredit those women who had contributed so greatly to Jesus' mission on earth.

These women, too, were apostles and disciples. Most often, they were simply ignored in the editing and rewriting of the Gospels. Mary, the mother of Jesus was reduced to perpetual virginity under the aegis of her son. But a woman as powerful as Mary of Magdala could not be completely disregarded.

Luke wrote she was the one out of whom came seven devils. Of what did these "devils" consist? Evil spirits, illness or just the power of a strong woman? Whatever the basis of the metaphor, devils carried the connotation of Satan, the dark. Thus, Mary was conveniently portrayed as a sinner, in league with dark, occult forces.

But one should always be aware that symbolism was a common element in the writings of those times.

Gardner proposes a different theory, in his *Bloodline of the Holy Grail*, utilizing this concept of symbolism: He postulates within the priesthood there were two groups; the seven priests of Light of the Menorah; and the seven opposing priests of darkness, the Demon priests. The chief scribe was Demon Priest number seven. All unmarried "Marys" (priestesses among women) were under the guardianship of the Chief Scribe until their marriage; at which time the seven devils (priests of darkness) can be said to have come out of them. This is to say, they were released from

28

that guardianship.

Other writers have seen the seven devils as illness, physical or psychological. The general consensus of opinion handed down through the centuries, however, envisioned the seven devils as representing sinfulness.

Therefore, Mary was conveniently labeled a sinner.

There appears to have been jealousy among the Apostles concerning Mary's relationship to Jesus. In the Gnostic *Gospel of Mary*, Peter says they know Jesus loved her more than the rest, and asks her to tell them the words that Jesus imparted to her alone.

In the *Gospel of Philip* she is called his "companion," implying a physical relationship between the two. Jesus was also reputed to have kissed her often on the mouth, incurring the displeasure of the disciples.

The *Gospel of Thomas* has Simon Peter saying "Let Mary leave us, for women are not worthy of life."

The Gospel writers, jealous of her power and intimacy with Jesus, did not accord Mary of Magdala the respect she was due. The Gospel writers, remember, were male Apostles. It was they who succeeded in continuing the lineage of Jesus' church according to Paul's interpretation. Paul insisted Jesus was Divine (male), the son of God the Father (male) and one with the Holy Spirit (also male, though seemingly sexless.)

After our journey of investigating and following her footsteps, I personally have become convinced that Mary of Magdala did indeed escape to the South of France with Jesus' closest friends. They would have brought with them that which, after reading the research of many scholars, I have come to believe were his true beliefs— simple directives for people to live lives of love and respect for God and each other.

In the country which was then known as Gaul, they spread the Word, later condemned as "heresy" by the Roman Church. From this source, as Simon Peter Fuller demonstrates through his tour groups to the area, evolve the strands of these "heresies," secret and hidden, which thread through history until today.

There is confusion as to where and when Mary Magdalene died and was buried. She is said to have died at age 60 in Sainte-Baume. She is also reputed to have died at Ephesus. Prior to her death, and after preaching the word of Jesus throughout the south of France, she is supposed to have lived many years in a cave as a hermit. There, she is said to have spent her time fasting and praying, naked except for her long hair, being gloriously lifted up to Heaven by angels seven times a day.

History books will tell you that Mary of Magdala simply disappeared. But what really seems to have happened is that she melted into the warp and weave of lore and legend, into the historic tapestry which is the colorful fabric of Southern France.

And so it was that here, in Les Saintes-Maries-de-la-Mer, standing in front of the two Marys in the little blue boat, we began in earnest to try to track her down.

LES-SAINTES-MARIES-DE-LA-MER:Saint Sarah

Chapter Five

SARAH, BLACK AND BEAUTIFUL

* * * * *

In the dark womb of her cave, in that extraordinary night of wonders, one wall began to glow mysteriously. As she reached her bed, sinking down upon its softness, she faced the strange luminescence.

No light could penetrate that comforting cavern. From whence its origin?

She rubbed her eyes in disbelief, excitement rising. It was beginning! Faces started to materialize within the dimness. They brightened for an instant, quickly faded away, transformed into new visages. Some were beautiful, some grotesque, dissolving one into the other so quickly they vanished on the very edge of recognition.

Who were these people? What did they want to tell her? Phantom figures, weaving softly, calling silently. Did she hear the words, or were they only in her mind? "Behold your lineage," a voice declared, softly whispering in her heart. What lineage? These shadowy images were not her noble mother or priestly father. She would have recognized them immediately, gladly welcoming them back into her arms.

"Behold!" the inner voice insisted. A female form emerged from the ghostly figures, pausing so she could be clearly seen. The woman was naked, enveloped in huge wings of gleaming feathers, fluttering softly, moving in an invisible wind. Her feet, birds' talons, were standing upon the back of two lions, which in turn were flanked by two owls. In her hand, she held a measure of grain.

31

"*I am Lillith.*" *The words rang in her heart.* "*I know the secret name of God. I hold the power of love, the strength of love, which lifts womankind from slavery and denigration. I am your ancestor. I am beautiful.*" *So saying, the apparition moved forward to stand near the woman's bed on the cave floor. She who was observing recoiled, shifting slightly away from the ghostly one.*

Another figure materialized in the soft light behind Lillith. Robed in shimmering gauze, stars formed a twinkling crown around her head. Clouds gathered by her feet. She was standing upon a globe, and in her hands she carried a crescent moon. "*I am Inanna,*" *the voice spoke in her heart,* "*the Goddess of all Heaven; of fertility, justice and healing. I existed long before you came to this world. You have always been part of me. I am beautiful.*" *The figure took her place beside Lillith, giving way to a third spirit coming forth.*

This woman's face shone like polished ebony. Her golden garment radiated tongues of flame as she drew it aside to reveal the dark crystal in her hands. "*I am Cybele,*" *she revealed silently. The crystal glowed with purple fire.* "*I am black, and I am beautiful, oh daughter of Jerusalem! I am your sister.*" *She too stepped forward to join the others near the bed.*

Another translucent Goddess entered in Cybele's wake. She was dark, with many breasts protruding from her chest. On her head she wore a crown resembling a tower. On the robe gathered at her waist shone figures of bulls, deer, goats and a bee, all glowing in pale blue radiance against the midnight cloth. In her right hand she carried a bow and arrow; her left hand rested upon the head of a bear. "*Do you not know me?*" *she addressed the living woman,* "*I am Artemis, the hunter, the bold side of your nature. I must be honored equally with the weak. I was born as a black stone, a meteor falling from the Heavens. I am black, and I am beautiful, oh my daughter.*" *She floated over to the side of the others.*

32

The last to emerge from the flickering shadows was a vaporous woman wearing a shining black robe and carrying a baby boy. A jeweled crown gleamed above her long dark hair. In her other hand she carried a scepter, ruby red, pulsing radiant light.

"Aye! I know you well, Isis!" cried the woman sitting on the bed. "I have served you in your temple. And I also know your son Horus. You are the eternal Mother, and you too know the secret name of God. You are black, you are beautiful, and you carry the secrets of death and rebirth within you. I welcome you, Isis, my mother! "

Braver now, she stood, straining to touch the Heavenly Madonna's skirt. But her hand, reaching through the wraithlike form, felt nothing but air.

"Come dance with us," chorused the Goddesses, " come join the dance of your mothers and sisters."

She moved into their circle. Their weaving phantom shapes danced about the lady, faster and faster, until all became a blur of ecstasy, and she sank exhausted to the cold stone floor, totally overcome.

When her eyes opened, they were gone.

What a miracle! she thought. Have I visited another world? Are these Goddesses awaiting me? That world must be coming closer, through the veil.

It cannot be very long now. Oh, such joyful awe fills my heart!

Elevated in spirit, but weary in body, she crawled back to her bed of furs, collapsing happily onto its welcoming softness.

* * * * *

I don't know how long we stood before the two Marys in the boat. Meditating on the meaning of the Magdalene, I had been swimming in an abyss of time. Fortunately, Karol tapped me on the shoulder.

"Let's go down into the crypt."

"Yes, of course. Let's go."

Crypts are wonderful places. Unlike the dark, dank, dripping dungeons the word crypt brings to mind (the result of Vampire movies, no doubt) those caverns underneath the altars of churches are sacred wombs of warmth and light. They are the shelters and protectors of especially venerated religious articles.

As we descended the stairs, a tide of warmth rose to envelop us. Scores of flickering candles momentarily distracted us from observing the blessed inhabitants of that cozy space.

Ah! There she was, dressed in royal purple, crowned in jeweled gold. Gypsy Saint, Gypsy Queen, a dark skinned Mary known as Sarah. Sprays of flowers in her arms, nose rubbed light by kisses of a million worshipers, this calm, beautiful, dark statue stood serenely against a background of discarded crutches and marble votive plaques.

Guidebooks will tell you her skin is dark because of the smoke of so many candles. Another error. The crypt's ceiling is stained by their smoke, but nothing else in that space is tainted with carbon. Sarah was painted brown because she was *supposed* to be brown. She is one of those mysterious Black Madonnas found in plentitude in southern France, and more rarely in other parts of the world.

Who are the Black Madonnas? Why are they black? They are turning up everywhere—I mean literally. Many are being plowed out of the ground, or found by animals. They seem to be clustered in Provence and Languedoc—the very lands the Marys and their companions made their home after coming to Gaul.

And what is the connection of Sarah, patron saint of Gypsies, to Egypt? Is it because the Gypsies were supposed to have come from Egypt? A common, but not likely, theory—because Gypsies actually came from India, not Egypt. There was, however, a busy trade route between Egypt and Palestine in Jesus' day. Egypt dominated the entire Mediterranean area until the

Greeks and Romans pushed them back through Palestine to the area we now know as Egypt.

Much of the culture remained, so it was not surprising that when the Marys came to France, their landing place was called the Island of Ra. The Egyptian sun god, Ra.

The original Sarah, wife of Abraham, spent some time in the Egyptian Pharaoh's household, until he discovered she was already married. Then he kicked both Sarah and Abraham out of Egypt. Hmmmm—I guess that could be one connection.

More likely the reason Sarah is venerated by the Gypsies is, that in the person of Helena, she held the title of "Sarah," religious rank of Cardinal among the tribe of Asher. As "Sarah," she was considered to be the mother of Gentiles and orphans.

Gentiles—those who came into the Hebrew faith from the ranks of outside unbelievers. Orphans—those needing the protection of a mother, people who need a home.

What could you tell us if you could speak? I mentally implored the statue of Sarah, who impassively returned my gaze. But did her eyes sparkle just a little? Maybe it was only the flickering candlelight.

I knew part of her metaphor. At the time of Christ, much esoteric, obscure spiritual knowledge had been derived from Egyptian culture, infiltrating Jewish philosophical systems. Mystical Hermetic Greek spiritual beliefs of that era also made their impressions on the Hebrews. These arcane views remained hidden from all but the initiated.

Goddess worship, with its elevation of the feminine, continued to weave its filaments among the people, continuing on into early Christianity.

From Egypt came Isis; the quintessential mother Goddess, the Wise One, often represented as black. Ancient traditions identify blackness with hidden wisdom.

From Greece arrived Artemis, the huntress, also frequently depicted as black. Diana, goddess of the moon and of the hunt, was her Roman counterpart.

As visible manifestations of secret knowledge, the Black Madonnas, Sarah among them, represent *Gnosis,* hidden knowledge, that secret personal experience of Enlightenment sought by the Gnostics, Bogomils, and Cathars. The belief of these religions in *Gnosis,* representing a personal and intimate connection with God without the intermediary of a priest, (or control by a powerful Roman hierarchy). As a result, they were ruthlessly persecuted by the Roman church as Christian heretics.

The Black Madonna hid her face, while the White Madonna, garbed in robes of purity, remained as a symbol of visible knowledge, patiently waiting to take her rightful place as the Bride in the Sacred Marriage of male and female.

Ean Begg, in his definitive work *The Cult of the Black Virgin*, quotes an earlier book by Robert Graves, *Mammon and the Black Goddess,* in which Graves sees the black virgin as symbolic of a new relationship between the sexes, promising a new bond between men and women, replacing the outdated patriarchal bond.

Perhaps the moment for it to happen is now, because at this time in history, there is a renewed upswell of the tide of feminine value, which has ebbed and flowed throughout the past.

From the era of Great Goddess,

—to suppression in Hebrew and Christian (and many other) religions,

—to resurgence in the Troubadours of twelfth century France,

—to repression again by the Roman Church,

—to the present flowering of feminine wisdom which is bringing balance back to our male dominated world,

— the rhythm has continued over the centuries in large waves and small ripples.

We are surfing a high wave. The Black Virgin, symbol of the mysterious, occult, powerful, dark side of the Feminine Principle, is being rediscovered. Many Black Madonnas, previously hidden by their faithful adherents, are coming to light. And along with this phenomenon, the White Virgin is manifesting in visions all over the world. It is a sign that the time for the restoration of the *unified* Holy Feminine has arrived. Wisdom—Sophia—Isis—Sarah—Virgin Mary—Mary of Magdala—all personifications of primal, feminine, creative energy, are coming together in wholeness at long last.

So why was Sarah in that boat with the Marys who came to France? How could they come *without* her? How could the Light move from Palestine to France without the Dark? One cannot exist without the other, for they are both parts of the Whole.

My attention returned abruptly to the crypt, to the statue of Sarah, which seemed to exude motherly love and warmth. It was the same feeling I experienced once, when that beautiful dark Indian woman known as Ammachi enveloped me in her arms in a huge tent in Santa Fe, during my recovery from breast cancer. I was but one of hundreds experiencing her embrace that day, but surely each of us received the same healing love, which she travels around the world sharing with all who find their way into her presence. A contemporary manifestation of the Goddess at work.

I kissed the hem of Sarah's purple robe, then moved past an altar housing some of her relics to a very mysterious plastic bubble against the opposite wall. Light reflecting from the banks of candles obscured what lay inside. Moving around to the edge, I could catch a glimpse of hidden treasure within.

"Karol! Come see!" Carrying her camera, with which she had been busily snapping photographs, Karol quickly joined me in the corner by that dark, shiny bubble. If you looked at just the right angle you could see a woman's head and shoulders, sculpted in black stone, rising out of blue waves, the whole sculpture placed under what resembled a huge protective plastic space visor.

"Those eyes! Karol, look at those eyes!" Staring out at the crypt from the beautiful stone face were two huge, oval, shining, almost alien, eyes. *Our Lady of the Unknown Universe,* I thought. A person could see the Cosmos in those eyes.

"I'm going to try to take her picture," I told Karol. Aiming the flash slightly off to the side, I hoped to catch the mysterious Lady on film. It worked, and it's a photograph I treasure above all others.

Awed by the encounter, we would have stayed in that warm, enfolding crypt much longer; but we knew it was time to leave. Happily, in a few days we would return. We were going to come back to witness a special ceremony, one which occurs only twice a year. In May, the statues of the two Marys in the boat, and Sarah, are reverently, amid much pomp and circumstance, carried from the church to the sea and back. In October, the two Marys alone are carried in the same kind of procession— and lucky us, we were going to be in Les Saintes-Maries-de-la-Mer to experience it!

Therefore, after lighting candles to remain with our prayers in the crypt, we left, feeling it was not goodbye, only *au revoir.*

Before departing the town to return to our *auberge,* however, I was buttonholed by an old Gypsy lady who, after reading my palm, pressed a small medal of St. Sarah into it.

"Pray to her, she will help you," the old Gypsy said in French, squeezing my hand around the medal, and patting it gently with a withered hand of her own.

"Pray to Sarah, she will help you," she repeated. Smiling a toothless grin, the crone turned in a swirl of colorful skirts, and was gone, leaving me dumbstruck, with St. Sarah in my palm.

All the rest of the day, and all that night, I heard the refrain from *The Song of Solomon:*

I am black, but I am beautiful, all ye daughters of Jerusalem.

running unceasingly through my mind. Its melody was reminiscent of a song of Wisdom I faintly remembered from long, long ago.

Chapter Six

THE GRAIL CHILD

* * * * *

Distant thunder awakened her from deep, dreamless sleep. Outside the cave's entrance, remote lightning dimmed night's bright stars, stabbing into the comforting darkness of her retreat.

Why tonight? The thought rose again. What is different about tonight, that visions come to dance with me? The Angels are often my company; I see them at each hour of prayer, when they lift my spirit to Heaven, nurturing me. But these visions are not angels.

She made her way once more to the opening, tasting the storm's acrid air as it approached across mountains blackening the horizon.

Why tonight? She shouted into the rising wind. Only thunder was her answer, more ominous now; louder, moving quickly toward her.

"Oh Yeshua, Yeshua!" she screamed in frustration at the rising storm. Is this you, in anger, trying to come near to me? I can feel your presence in this wild night. Do you approach me, or do I dream? I can no longer trust my senses!

Lightning split a tree in the forest directly below the cliff face where she stood. The reverberating thunderclap nearly lifted her off her feet, sending her scurrying back into the safety of the cavern.

I shall have to wait for my answer, she reasoned, breathlessly sinking down upon the bed. *This cannot be the Master. His anger has never touched me. Blessed Yeshua will certainly not come to me in fear and trembling, but in peace and love.*

Again she returned to the memory of that other storm, which had cast them upon these shores thirty years earlier. They had been carrying two hidden treasures: one beneath her skirts about to be born; the other securely enclosed in a wooden chest. Scarcely had the survivors washed ashore on this welcome Isle, when the sodden chest came bobbing onto the beach as if drawn by sea horses in a chariot.

Laughing lightly, she remembered one of the pink birds settling upon it, pecking at its lock with curious beak. *Shoo!* she had remonstrated. *Silly bird, you do not know the treasure within— you are like a flea on the back of an elephant!* The curious bird flapped away as her companions, with the last of their strength, dragged the chest high up the beach to safety.

Once the storm abated, they had buried it in a place near a stand of tall bushes; the same spot where they later built a shrine to celebrate their safe arrival, and to conceal it.

For they knew the greatest treasures of Israel lay within that cedar chest: the golden Menorah, Chalice and Plate from the Temple in Jerusalem, smuggled into their safekeeping by their secret sympathizer, Pontius Pilate.

"Take these," he had said. "Bring them safely to Gaul; for they are truly your sacred treasure, and must not fall into the soiled hands of corruption. Joseph of Arimathea will carry them further, to Britannia, far from here. And in time beyond that, they will travel west across the ocean, bringing enlightenment to new lands."

Yeshua must have been protecting them, she thought, and his loved ones as well; for all had survived the perilous journey. And it was no more than two Sabbaths after their arrival that the other treasure was born. It was a boy. She

40

wrapped him in her own soft clothing, laid him in a bed of grasses and named him Josephes. White horses and black bulls had come to gently nuzzle the infant, carefully guarded by his delighted sister and brother.

Yes, she mused, so many years afterwards; how different from the birth of his father! No bright star in the heavens, no adoring Wise Men bearing gifts. But another child-king, carrying his lineage, was certainly born in this foreign land.

Suddenly a bright light burst into her eyes, diffusing brilliance throughout the cave. In its center a beautiful golden chalice encrusted with precious jewels pulsed with radiance almost too resplendent to envision. Bearing the glorious chalice was a small child. Her child.

"Josephes!" she exclaimed in awe, blinded by the brilliance. "Why are you, my precious, the bearer of such a treasure?"

* * * * *

It was time to leave Les-Saintes-Maries-de-la Mer. Regretfully, because this sunny, festive little town had quickly found a special place in our hearts. It was a place that seemed both a beginning and an ending, though I didn't quite know why. But as I just mentioned, parting was softened by the knowledge we would return a week later, to witness the festival in which the Saints Mary are brought down to visit the sea from which they had arrived.

Therefore it was with light hearts that Karol and I turned our little green Renault north towards Arles, and west to Siran in Languedoc. There, we planned to meet Simon Peter Fuller and his friend Ross to share a week of exploration in Cathar country. Peter, you may remember, was our guide to Sacred Sites in England

41

the year before. He had declared himself just as eager as I to visit these historic places linking to the Magdalene.

Although just about everyone knows Arles as Van Gogh's home for a period of time, few people are aware of the really special place in Arles I wanted to visit.

Alyscamps is a pre-Christian Celtic cemetery, so sacred to the Celts who had been driven north from France by the Romans, that they were said to have placed important people in barrels with burial money and floated them down the Rhône to Alyscamps to be interred in this holy ground.

"I wonder how many actually made it," Karol speculated, navigating the car dangerously around hundreds of little trucks and temporary stalls clogging narrow streets. It was market day in Arles, and the whole town seemed abloom with flowers, spicy aromas, crafts, foods, colorful fabrics, livestock, pets, and people of all ages, sorts and kinds. Lots of people. Scads of people. Tons of people. Thousands of people.

"Probably more made it than their money did," I replied, as she braked to avoid an old man crossing the street, a squawking brown hen firmly in his grip. (I sincerely hoped he was taking it home to lay eggs or be a pet.) "There have always been scoundrels. Whoops, turn right—there's a sign for the Alyscamps."

Karol skillfully berthed the Renault into a tiny parking lot just outside iron gates surrounding the ancient cemetery. Those might as well have been doors to another world.

Like Alice in Wonderland falling down the rabbit hole, we walked through the gates to enter a world of fantasy; but ours was a silent, mysterious cosmos pervaded by spirits and memories.

Only a fraction of its former size, the cobbled Roman road led us toward a ruined Romanesque church at the other end. As we picked our way leisurely among stone sarcophagi lining the road on both sides, we found a sign indicating where Van Gogh sat to paint his famous painting of the Alyscamps. A copy of the painting, permanently imprinted on a historic marker, showed a brilliant, tree-shaded pathway with a couple strolling by colorful sarcophagi—a far cry from the misty, gray fall day we were experiencing. Our atmosphere was far more in keeping with shadows of the past; shadows which crowded, alive and whispering, close around our shoulders.

Touching the lichen-stained, gray, cold stone coffins, we could not help but wonder who had once lain within. Celtic Warrior? Queen? Priest or Priestess? Beloved husband or wife? Ancient seer, or soldier too young to die?

"Oh, Karol," I burbled, "if only the stones could talk!"

Duh! Of course we can't speak their language. Nevertheless, memories of ancient stories bubbled up unbidden in my imagination, as we continued walking the tree-lined cobble road toward the ruined church. Perhaps the stones *were* talking, in their own way, to people willing to listen.

Once inside the church, we were in yet another world. Dim, eerie, nearly empty. Soft light filtering through a colored glass window painted golden the cover of a sarcophagus below it. The lid was carved with a Celtic cross. Nearby, a perfectly preserved stone coffin bore corner sculptures of Egyptian faces in full headdress. Other sarcophagi bore images of angels, saints, spirals, waves. There were even huge burial jars in corners of the ruined building. Judging from the various cultural motifs exhibited here, this was most certainly a very cosmopolitan burial ground. We were not alone in that silent place, although no other people were there. A photograph I took by the Celtic cross showed an angel, painted in light, on the wall behind. I could swear I had not seen it there before.

On our way out through the roofless foyer, a broken, black stone column seemed to call us from an arched niche. Why would a broken stone column merit such a prestigious showcase? Then I remembered Artemis had been discovered as a black stone, fallen from Heaven. Was this a tribute to a primal Goddess? Was this a Black Virgin? Was this another face of Mary Magdalene?

Musings of this sort occupied my mind and our conversation most of the time we strolled the Roman road back

43

towards bustling Arles on the other side of the iron gates. Had Mary Magdalene visited this sacred place on her travels through Provence? Surely she must have, because the mighty Rhône River, major pre-Christian highway between the Mediterranean and the British Isles, flowed by these Elysian Fields (*Alyscamps*) in her timetime, as it does now.

The Rhône was a major tin route between Cornwall and Palestine. Thousands of years before Christ, copper ore had been mined in Jordan, and sent to southern Israel for smelting in the Beersheba Valley. There, rich alluvial soil supported a larger population, with both a labor force to mold copper into tools and weapons, and a market to sustain the industry.

But copper is soft. Someone discovered that alloying tin with copper produced bronze, a much harder material, and thereby launched the Bronze Age. Since no tin was found in the Palestine area, a trade route developed from the mines of the British Isles to the copper smelting area of Israel. Two routes were favored: a sea voyage through the Straits of Gibraltar, and a river route up the Rhône through Gaul.

"Wasn't Joseph of Arimathea a tin merchant?" questioned Karol in response to my verbal observations.

"Yes, apparently he was," I answered. "And there are legends he took Jesus with him to Glastonbury, in England. But I think it is more reasonable he took Mary Magdalene's child Jesus the Younger, or else Josephes, the Grail Child, instead."

"Whoa, Cinnie, back up. Who was Josephes?"

"The baby boy born to Mary Magdalene and Jesus shortly after she arrived in Provence."

"But why do you call him the Grail Child?"

"If the many scholars who have researched this are right, he is called the Grail Child because he is the *Sang Réal* (Holy Blood) of Jesus' Kingly House of David. In Medieval times, the words Sang Réal became mis-translated into Holy Grail. When it is said Joseph of Arimathea brought the Holy Grail to Glastonbury, it means he may have brought the child of Jesus there."

"But how did Joseph of Arimathea get the child of Jesus to go with him?"

"It's simple, when you know that Joseph of Arimathea was really James, the younger brother of Jesus. He may have been one of the people accompanying the Marys to Provence in that boat. He came through that way often, because it was along his tin route."

"The younger brother of Jesus? Wasn't Jesus' mother supposed to be forever virgin?"

"So some religions declare, but there is evidence in the Bible and from historical writings near that time, that Mary and Joseph had more children after Jesus was born."

"OK, but even if that is true, if his name was James why did they call him Joseph?"

"Good question," I laughed. This is one example of why so many people have misunderstood the Bible. The ancient Hebrews had a habit of naming people with certain special responsibilities after their forefathers. That's why the "Marys," the priestesses among women, were named after Miriam (Mary) the sister of Moses."

"I knew that."

"But most people do not know the many other names used as job descriptions among the Hebrews. For example, the first in line to the throne of the royal House of David was called the "David". The next in line was called the "Joseph." So Jesus' ("David's") next younger brother James is called the "Joseph." That's why Jesus' father was also called "Joseph," since he was second in line to the throne. It was through his father that Jesus claimed to be in line for the throne of David. This royal genealogy was very important to the Hebrews, waiting for a messiah, even though the Davidic monarchy had not been in power for generations."

"Pretty confusing," Karol muttered.

"You're right," I agreed. "But there's more. Joseph wasn't from Arimathea any more than Jesus was from Nazareth. Arimathea

45

can be seen as deriving from "Rama" (height) and "Theo" (God). It can translate into 'Divine Highness.' And James, the "Joseph" was in competition with Jesus for the Kingship until he went over to his brother's side."

We had reached the car.

"Do you suppose we can just *drive* now?" Karol was ready to let that subject go for a while. She navigated us through the now magically cleaned up streets, through the maze of alleys dead-ending at the river, finally ascending the bridge which spans the mighty Rhône.

Crossing that huge river, it was easy to imagine boats loaded with tin riding the current south; and boats loaded with copper or other goods, sailing north, or being dragged along the banks by beasts of burden— perhaps raw manpower. By comparison, how easy it was for us, driving effortlessly along the AutoRoute towards Languedoc, the Land of the Cathars!

Our thoughts turned forward now, to arriving at the *gîte* (rental cottage) we had secured through the magic of the Internet. The cottage nestled, waiting for us, in the heart of Languedoc's fertile wine country.

After skirting the Mediterranean coast, we moved inland, through the ancient town of Béziers (where 20,000 or more men, women and children— the town's entire population— were killed in the 12th century by the Roman church in its persecution of heretics), and westward to the little town of Siran.

There, we planned to settle in for a week, joining Peter and Ross to explore medieval Carcassonne, mysterious Rennes-le-Château, Cathar castles and prehistoric Magdalenian (don't you love it? She's everywhere!) cave art in underground caverns.

We were looking forward to an exciting time.

ALYSCAMPS:
Broken Stone Coumn in Niche

Chapter Seven

PAUL

* * * * *

Long she sat, eyes blinded but mind clear. At last she realized the full meaning of the responsibility Yeshua had given her. His Word, through his seed and her lips, was the real treasure, not the golden treasures of the Temple. Those, James had indeed carried on to Britannia.

Fully comprehending his Word was the quest for the Golden Chalice held aloft by Josephes. The child and the chalice—they were one and the same!

She remembered when he had entrusted her with the mission. They had been standing outside the walls of Qumran, taking their parting. He, to travel towards the east, teaching amidst the mountains; she, to flee with the children to safety in Gaul.

"We may never meet again in this lifetime," he had told her gently, looking deep into her weeping eyes. "But we are one soul. We shall be reunited some day in the House of our Creator."

Tears overflowed onto her cheeks. She wiped them away with her hair, just as she had dried his feet at his Anointing. He kissed her wet face, pulling her closer.

"Let not your heart be sad," he whispered, "for you have much work to do. You must carry my message to all people, just as you carry my seed within your womb. You must tell them the greatest secret of all, that we are all sons

49

and daughters of God; and that Love is the sword of truth. Everyone has the capability of being as I am, in direct communion with the Creator, with whom all things are possible."

She nodded mutely, too overcome with emotion to speak.

"And then, when you have accomplished this, you are destined to undertake another mission. It is too soon for you to understand what I ask of you."

She regarded him, eyes filled with questions, but he pushed her away to face him squarely, seriously, holding her firmly by the shoulders.

"Beware, my love, my wife," he cautioned, "the road is full of dangers. Many would corrupt my words, bending them to their own desires. The truth you speak will also be your peril.

"Especially, take care to avoid Saul. You are a thorn in his side. I will meet him soon, on the road to Damascus. I shall call down the Light and blind him. After that, seeing with new eyes, he will change his name to Paul and vow to support our cause— but he still will be serving his own purpose. Beware his ambition!"

How prophetic had been Yeshua's words! She shuddered, remembering her later meeting with Paul in the Elysian Fields of Gaul.

Paul had traveled west from Italy to gain converts for his Romanized Christian church. She had led her friends across Gaul's marshlands to the ancient Celtic cemetery, preaching the message of Yeshua to crowds along the way.

By the black stone she had paused, remembering the Goddess, her mother.

"Why stand you there worshipping a stone?" Paul had suddenly appeared from within the temple, followed by twelve men armed with daggers.

"Do you not know it is forbidden to worship idols?"
He spat at the stone.

"I do not worship, I remember," she had responded, looking up at his angry face.

"Heretic! He shouted. You go around preaching our Yeshua was not the Son of God! We know he is Divine, God incarnate."

"You are wrong!" she had cried defiantly. "Yeshua never said he was the only begotten Son of God. He said we are ALL Divine. All of us are part of God! We need no priests to speak for us! We can do as he did, even perform miracles."

"How would you know?" He snarled. "You are only a woman. If you prove your words, I will allow your mission."

She smiled now in the darkness of the cave, remembering her moment of power. Years had faded away and she was once more back in the cemetery with Paul.

"See this poor pup that limps over to us, licking our hands for favors? By the grace of God I shall heal him!" she announced loudly.

Derisive laughter from the men, at the brashness of her words. But they all crowded around as she sat down upon the cobbled road, gathering the shivering puppy into her lap.

"There, there," she crooned, caressing the little dog's face. The puppy stopped shivering, settling himself comfortably in her skirts. Moving her fingers in little circles over his body, she found an area of distress near his rear haunch. She cupped her hands over the spot, closed her eyes and breathed long, deep breaths, allowing energy to flow through her fingers.

Almost immediately the puppy yelped and hopped to the ground, tossing his head, jumping up repeatedly to lick her face.

"You see?" She rose to her feet, smoothing her garment and pushing back her hair. "No limping now!

51

Martha, please give the dog some bread and cheese. The poor thing is hungry."

Paul stalked over to the side of the road. Furiously, he scrubbed a line with the toe of his sandal in dirt next to the paving.

"See this line?" he demanded. "To the west of it is the land of Oc. To the east lies Rome and Greece and Corinth. I concede to you the western portion. I shall leave you among those savages. There is more than enough work for me to do in civilized lands to the east! Who would believe what a woman says anyway?"

Turning abruptly, he stormed out of the sacred cemetery, followed by twelve angry men.

She laughed aloud now, as she had laughed then. Paul had been defeated by a woman! And she had become more determined than ever to carry out Yeshua's mission among the people in Gaul.

* * * * *

It was a long drive west towards Siran. We took turns at the wheel, stopping at clean and comfortable rest areas to walk around, change drivers and get a breath of fresh air in the warm autumn afternoon.

Driving was a good opportunity for talk. Our conversation in the Alyscamps had piqued Karol's curiosity. She wanted to know more.

"Cinnie, you have studied the recent research about these early Christian times. If Joseph was really James, Jesus was the David, and Marys were priestesses, who was this man Paul?"

I laughed, watching reedy bushes stream by. "Paul was just Paul, except of course he was born Saul and later changed his name."

"Sure, on the road to Damascus, everybody knows that."

"Yes, but there's a lot about Paul people don't know."

"He was born in Tarsus, wasn't he?"

"That's right," I agreed, "but Tarsus wasn't in Israel. It was in Greece. Paul wasn't a Jew by birth, although he claimed to be of the tribe of Benjamin."

Karol was studying a car riding really close behind us. "They don't give people much room, do they?"

"Uh huh. Maybe we're going too slow for them."

"We're doing the speed limit."

At that instant, the car pulled out and passed us, disappearing quickly around a curve ahead.

"Wow! Reminds me of New York City taxi drivers. Really fast, but really good. I close my eyes in New York taxis, but they never hit anything."

"Let's hope," she sighed. "Anyway, what's this about Paul not being a Jew?"

"Well, he passed himself off as a Pharisee, one of the learned ones, but he seems to have been a bit of a con man. His follower, Luke, wrote that he studied under a great Pharisee teacher named Gamaliel."

"I thought the Pharisees were hypocrites. Doesn't it say that in the Gospels?"

"Yes, but you must remember the books that were included in the New Testament were only a few among thousands of documents relating to the life of Jesus. And only ones that supported Paul's view of Jesus' teachings were chosen to be in the Bible. The Pharisees got a raw deal in those Gospels."

Another car zoomed by, and yet another, chasing it. Karol just shrugged this time, urging me to continue.

"The Pharisees were actually respected as a dedicated group who stood for their religious ideals. They opposed persecution of Jesus' followers. They were law abiding, and cared for the needs of the poor."

"I always get the Pharisees and the Sadducees mixed up."

"I did too," I agreed, "until I started studying this thing seriously. The Sadducees were priests and aristocrats at the time

53

of Jesus. They differed from the Pharisees in that they believed in literal interpretation of the Bible, rejecting oral laws and traditions. They also did not believe in an afterlife and the coming of a Messiah."

"Which group liked Jesus?" Karol was mentally sorting them out.

"The Pharisees. Jesus and his group were among them. Everyone was waiting for a Messiah then, kind of like what's happening now, as we begin a new millennium. But in those times, Messiah didn't just mean a God/King, it meant a royal warrior who would save Israel from the Romans."

"I guess it was a political mishmash; the Romans, the Pharisees, the Sadducees...."

"Yes, and add to that the Zealots, who wanted to get rid of the Romans, using guerilla tactics. Political intrigue isn't something new to this century."

Karol laughed ruefully. "That's for sure."

A few quiet moments of thought, about the morass of current politics, while scenery slipped smoothly by, and cars continued to pass us, fading quickly into the distant horizon.

I wondered if political intrigue is part and parcel of the human character. Can we ever possibly have real peace? It seems to me history is not linear, it is circular; or more precisely, spiral. We come around again and again, to the same issues in different times. The French have a saying that translates "The more things change, the more they stay the same." The same problems erupt, just different stage sets, different costumes, different eras.

"But back to Paul, Karol," I finally ventured. "He wanted to be known as a Pharisee, but first he worked for the Sadducee High Priest as a strong arm man, harassing and persecuting the followers of Jesus. It is reported, among other things, he threw James down a flight of stairs at the Temple."

"I wasn't aware of that little nastiness, but I did know he persecuted the Christians."

54

"Yes, but he was also an adventurer who saw an opportunity to become a big celebrity. He never met Jesus while Jesus was alive. But on that road to Damascus after being hit by lightning he saw a vision of the risen Christ, and that was his opportunity. He became a Roman citizen, changed his name to Paul in honor of Sergius Paulus, the Roman governor of Cyprus, all the better to promote his idea of Jesus' teachings in the Roman dominated world."

"Do you mean he didn't believe what Jesus said?"

"Not exactly as Jesus said it. Paul saw Jesus as the Mystic Christ, God Incarnate. It evolved from a concept he encountered in Arabia of a Heavenly Messiah who incarnates, dies and is resurrected to save humanity. Jesus never claimed to be Divine any more than the rest of us. Yet Paul believed in all the good things Jesus taught—about how to relate to mankind, even if he excluded womankind. But Paul could not exclude Mary Magdalene. She was too important a figure in Jesus' life to ignore."

"Did they ever meet?"

"Yes, probably, in Jerusalem before she went to France; and very possibly several times thereafter. It is said she challenged him. Certainly her mission created crowds of converts to her version of Jesus' teachings in France, while Paul kept pretty much to the lands east of there.

"Paul was very charismatic, attracting many converts. But the original followers of Jesus accused him of founding a new church, and disowned him."

"He sounds like quite a guy, lots of *chutzpah*."

"I guess so, because it seems he invented much of his own biography in order to facilitate his missionary activities."

We had crossed a boundary between departments of Provence and Languedoc, turning away from the sea towards Béziers. Navigating began to take precedence over conversation. By e-mail, Philippe and Margaret Jackson, hosts at our *gîte* in Siran, had given us directions to the cottage, named LeThéron.

55

Circling our way through Béziers proved more difficult than anticipated. I drove into Béziers, around Béziers, through Béziers, looking for the obscure signs to Carcassonne, which Philippe had promised would be found there. These medieval streets were built for ox carts, not modern cars! A fellow next to us at one of the many turns yelled at me for being too close to him—how could you not be? We nearly touched side view mirrors, but the stream of French he hurled our way, accelerating out of our vicinity, was magnificent—and I was glad I couldn't understand the slang.

Finally, however, Karol's excellent map interpretation got us on the right road. Soon we entered the little town of Siran, turned right at the second road past the *Mairie* and followed the electric lines through vineyards and valleys to the delightful 200-year-old stone cottage called LeThéron.

CARCASSONNE:
Moat and Bridge to the City

SIRAN:
LeTheron, our Home for a Week

Chapter Eight

LeTHÉRON, IN THE
LAND OF OC

* * * * *

Her delight in remembering besting Paul at Alyscamps gradually faded into bewilderment, then rose again in anger at his self-serving ambition. Brushing back her tousled hair, her ragged fingernails scratched three angry red lines across her forehead. She did not even notice.

Hypocrite! Why had Paul been so defiant, so arrogant in his interpretation of The Way? Yeshua had said it simply and often—"Love God with all your heart and soul and love your neighbor as yourself."

James— the Joseph— who succeeded to leadership of the Way, had denounced Paul for trying to start an entirely new church. James was right! That was not Yeshua's desire. He wanted only to perfect their sacred Hebrew religion. She knew that as God's own truth.

"Yeshua!" she blurted his name into the darkness. "This was not your Word! Why did you allow it to be recast? Why did you not appear to Paul and chastise him? You left only me, and those of your friends who came with me, to spread your message.

"We are old now. Most of us have left this earth. Many people have heard our voices, and they follow you—

but will they carry on the faith you brought them, the fulfillment of the Law, without us?

"Yeshua! Can you hear me?

"Yeshua! Have we failed you?"

Perhaps she fantasized, but she thought she saw a dim outline of his cherished face in the darkness, and the whisper of his voice in her heart.

"My love, my love," she thought she heard him say; "lay down this burden. You have done enough. You have planted the seeds. They will flower without your nurture. You must understand there will be many who will misinterpret my words. Those who follow me in simplicity and truth will be declared heretic. They, who wrongfully claim to be my believers, will persecute them. It will be so. You cannot prevent it. But you can help to heal it."

"Yeshua!" she cried again, wishing with all her soul to bring his image into reality. "Why must it be so? What am I to do?"

But the likeness faded, the voice stilled within her, and she was left alone once more; a frail, yearning figure, no longer content in the cave she had called home for thirty years.

* * * * *

Margaret and Philippe were waiting to greet us at the farm, which has become their home.

"We were worried about you," said Margaret. "We thought you were lost."

"Just never send us through Béziers again!" I begged jokingly. "There must be another way to get here."

"Of course, you can use the back roads. I'll show you on the map," offered Philippe.

"Never mind that now," interrupted Margaret, "they need to get to the grocery store quickly, because it will be closed tomorrow. Everything closes down on Sunday."

"Right. Just unload your suitcases here by the stairs to your cottage. I'll take you in, give you the key, and you can be off to the store in town. You can't miss it. There's only one. Don't mind Iggy." By this he meant the chubby little gray-muzzled black dog wiggling for attention at our feet.

Finally satisfied he had been properly acknowledged, Iggy loped off with Margaret towards the main house, while Philippe helped us bring our belongings down several stone steps to our future home.

The house had once been quarters for two farm families. Now lovingly restored by Philippe and Margaret, this 200-year-old stone cottage contained two separated upstairs sleeping apartments. Beneath them, on the ground level were a modern kitchen, a cozy living room with fireplace, and a den furnished with a television set.

We were delighted. It was just what we had imagined and hoped for— rustic, authentic; but comfortable, in a setting of vineyards, and a view south all the way to the Pyrenees mountains. So Country French! So comfortable! The stuff of dreams and fantasy.

Karol and I chose the nearer twin bedroom and bath, up a flight of twisting, original stone stairs from the kitchen. Peter and Ross could have the other end of the house, we decided.

Almost immediately, we were off to the only grocery in Siran. Obviously, we didn't know the system. At home, vegetables are weighed at checkout. The patient checkout lady courteously handed all our vegetables back to another woman, who returned to the vegetable section to weigh them. While she was doing that, I tried to add two loaves of delicious looking French bread that were lying next to the counter.

"Oh non, Madame," laughed the checkout madame in accents of her local French dialect. "They belong to her—*à elle."* She gestured to another smiling lady, waiting patiently while our vegetables were being weighed. "You must buy bread at the bakery. La boulangerie."

"Ah, oui," I replied as best I could. *"Pardonnez-moi. Mais où est la boulangerie?* Where is the bakery?"

Since our inability to follow the complicated verbal directions was entirely apparent, the kind ladies shepherded us to the door, pointing the way down the street. We had to park our car by the bank, then walk up an alley too narrow to admit cars, to the bakery. There we met another lady we had seen at the little grocery.

Small town. By Church time tomorrow everyone would know we were the two dingbat American ladies staying at the Jacksons' place. Nevertheless, they would speak kindly of us. I have never known a French person to respond unkindly to my bumbling ineptitude.

Arriving back at LeThéron, we unloaded supplies of local bounty in the kitchen and invited Margaret and Philippe to join us in sampling the bottle of delicious wine they had left upon our table, a welcoming gift bottled by their friend at the local co-op.

Like many Englishmen who yearn for a place of their own in a sunny, warm Mediterranean climate, the Jacksons bought this property in the Minervois section of Languedoc. It is an area that was formerly parceled out to retiring Roman military officers as reward for their service.

The old estate had been badly in need of repairs. Philippe set about restoring the main farmhouse, which became their home, then refurbished the cottage where we were staying. Margaret, with the aid of an electric jackhammer, had pounded the rocky soil into submission, planting gardens, trees and grass where wild scrub previously grew. It had taken a few years, but now the four stone buildings of the *domaine* were surrounded with delightful landscaping, and the *gîte* was fully booked for the rental season.

Over wine, we discussed the reason for our being here and the places we planned to visit the coming week. Our hosts answered all sorts of questions we had accumulated en route.

"Why is it I can't seem to pronounce many of the place names we see on road signs?" I asked. "They don't follow the rules of pronunciation I learned in school."

"Because the place names here still reflect the ancient language of Oc."

"Oc?"

"Oc, the Occident, was formerly a country stretching from the Pyrenees across the south of France all the way to the Adriatic Sea," explained Philippe. That is how this particular Department of France became known as Languedoc. *Langue d'Oc.* The translation is 'Language of Oc'. Oc meant the West, as opposed to the center of civilization at that time, further east in Egypt, Palestine, Turkey and Greece."

"OK, since we're into language of road signs, what does *Bis* mean?"

"The scenic route," laughed Margaret. "Once when we were waiting for long overdue guests, we found out they followed the route marked *Bis*. Never do that unless you have lots of spare time."

"One more thing, " Karol piped up, "what are those yellow diamond road signs?" Nobody really knew. They didn't seem to mean anything. Later we discovered they are placed in areas where the main road has the right of way. Doesn't the main road always have the right of way? Not in France, I guess.

On a more serious note, I asked Philippe about the Cathars. We were close to the heart of what is known as Cathar Country. He told us they were a religious sect in the 12th and 13th century, persecuted by the Roman Catholic church as heretics. They had many beliefs similar to those of the Gnostics, with whom Christianity coexisted comfortably during the first century.

Primarily, they believed in duality of good and evil. All earthly concerns were evil. All spiritual concerns were good. People were good spirits imprisoned in bad bodies. One did not attain unity with the Divine through ritual, but through a secret knowing, or *Gnosis*, a direct communion with God, and a life free from almost any pleasures of the flesh.

"Why did the Roman Church consider them heretics?" Karol asked.

For one thing, they didn't need priests to intercede for them," I offered from my cursory study of the subject. "And they did not recognize the Pope as head of true Christianity."

"They honored women as well as men among those they called *parfaits*," added Philippe, "Those were the people who had attained the highest degree of other-worldliness; they were the perfect ones."

"It seems they were closer to Essene and Gnostic beliefs than Pauline doctrine," I continued. "Closer to the original preaching of Jesus. I wonder if the ministry of the Magdalene was their original source."

"Possibly," agreed Philippe, "but in any case early in the 13th century they were mostly wiped out by Catholic mercenaries. You will learn more about them when you visit the famous Cathar castles near here."

It had been a long driving day, and Peter and Ross were due to arrive the next afternoon, so Karol and I excused ourselves and climbed the ancient stairs to our room.

A little later, I lay in crisp linen sheets, gazing out a square window at the moon. Thinking of the many people who had lived in this old house, I wondered about all the stories those massive stone walls could tell.

OK, all you who lived here before, you are welcome to visit me tonight in my dreams, if you are in the Light, I thought, drifting off to sleep.

Perhaps I should not have extended such an open invitation. In the middle of the night I was awakened by sharp pain in my left knee. I limped to the bathroom, so as not to awaken Karol in the other bed, and turned on the light. There, on the skin on the inside of my knee were three parallel red scratches, rapidly becoming welts. I put some soothing aloe lotion on them and went back to bed. *Now what could that be all about?* I wondered for a while, then fell deeply back into slumber.

64

Chapter Nine

MEDIEVAL MYSTERIES

* * * * *

No sleep will come to comfort me this night, she concluded, long before dawn. This night's darkness is filled with miracles and mysteries. I am no longer content to spend my life a contemplative in this hermitage! Yet my heart feels lighter, closer to my beloved, and the blood courses faster through my veins. Her fragile body began to tremble with unaccustomed energy.

"Yeshua!" She called to him in the strength of her mind, this time expecting him to answer. And in her mind she heard him once again.

"I come to guide you," he answered. "Trust me."

"Why do you bring me, this night of all nights, these fantasies, these memories of times long past?" she demanded of him to know.

Gravely, he responded. "The Law requires that before you come to join me, you must fully understand the purpose of your existence. You have seen memories of the past, and have come to know what part your living plays in the present. But you have yet to comprehend your role in the future. It will be made clear to you."

"When?" She feared there would be but little time.

"Rest, my love." His voice was smiling at her impatience. "Be at peace and learn from that which will unfold."

In expectation now, instead of fear, she lay back and closed her eyes once more.

Without seeming to take another breath, she found herself in a brightly decorated building. How beautiful! How astonishing! What could this place be?

It looks like a temple, she thought, but very different from the ones I know. Gazing at the wealth of paintings and statues, she saw rich colors and adornments totally foreign to the humble homes of her faithful companions, or her own familiar cave. Even the windows, admitting delicately hued sunbeams through deeply colored patterns of glass, fragmented everything they touched into bursts of color.

Could this be a palace? Though it is beautiful, it does not appear like anything I have seen in the palace of King Herod. No, it seems more like a place of worship. But of what kind? All these statues appear to be held in great reverence, but they do not look familiar. We Jews do not believe in idols; although those of us who hold the Goddess in our hearts honor images of Isis.

She glanced at the many benches for crowds of people to rest upon, inside the body of this room. There were no balconies or outer courts for women, such as in the Hebrew temples. Everyone seemed to be welcome to worship here together, men and women alike. Just as we, the Faithful, worship in our humble houses and simple churches, she reflected.

Could this be a temple of that future time Yeshua promised to reveal? Is this what our simple churches in the Land of Oc are to become? Such a concept was inconceivable, overwhelming to the point of disbelief. "No!" she cried soundlessly. "Impossible!"

From her position near the door, she noticed two couples entering. They were dressed in clothing unlike anything she had ever seen. Amazingly, before she could move aside, they walked right through her! Glancing down, she saw she had no body, just a total awareness of being in that place, as if inside a brilliant dream, looking out at the world.

Wonder of wonders!

In that amazing room, under a celestial blue dome sparkling with golden stars, was an altar. Its front panel bore a painting of a woman with long auburn hair, kneeling in sorrow by a cave.

That could not possibly be a likeness of Isis, she determined, for Isis would be shown with a child in her arms, not kneeling in sorrow. The Queen of Heaven kneeling in sorrow? Never. Ah! —there she is, beside the altar, holding baby Horus in her arms. And yes, she wears the red robe and cloak of black. But why so fair of skin? Isis is darkly beautiful.

That other statue on the opposite side of the altar—it might be Osiris, beloved husband of Isis. He also holds the babe in his arms. But he, like she, he is too fair in color. So heavily bearded and clad in flowing robes of gold! They look more Jewish than Egyptian. Something is very wrong. Is this really a vision, or just my fantasy?

Why, since everything is so strange— why is it so unsettlingly familiar?

Yeshua, help me understand, she prayed silently.

Fascinated, she continued to inspect the room. Many people, painted onto the walls and sculpted into statues! Who are they? In its place of honor near the altar, a statue of a young man carrying a lily and a baby in his arms stood upon a pedestal adorned with images of beautiful ladies. On a wall adjacent to him, a sad young woman, standing upon a shelf supported by cherubs, held a cross close to her breast.

A cross? That instrument of death and torture? She shuddered, remembering her greatest day of sorrow.

By the door where the visitors had entered, a hideous demon knelt, supporting a basin of water shaped like a shell. Above him four beautiful angels stood in front of a rose

67

decorated symbol, much like a cross. That cross again! Good and Evil standing close together! It was a relief to observe Good standing superior to Evil.

Behind her—oddly, she did not need to turn to see—was a large painting of a man on a rose-strewn hillside, surrounded by people raptly listening to his words. Kneeling in adulation by his side was the woman from the altarpiece, the one with long copper hair. She too was dressed in the robes of Isis!

Her gaze drifted to the bottom of the panel. Beneath the crowd's feet the artist had painted a bag of money, torn open to exhibit gold inside.

One of the women who had entered the church was pointing to it, talking to her companion in a foreign language. Mysteriously, she who was observing without body, was able to understand their conversation.

"Could this bag of money refer to the treasure that Mary and Joseph of Arimathea were supposed to have brought from the Temple in Jerusalem?" one of the women asked her friend.

"Could be," responded the other woman turning away from the painting. "This place is full of symbols and tricks. But in my opinion, the real treasure was secret knowledge that Mary Magdalene and Jesus had children. The Church would need to suppress such information."

"There might be deeper meanings in these symbols, as well," added the first woman. "Maybe connections to the Holy Grail."

Mary Magdalene? Joseph of Arimathea? Why do these people speak of me, and James, the brother of Yeshua? More baffled than ever, she peered around the room. Instantly, she found herself facing the statue of the sad woman hugging the cross. Underneath was a plaque saying "Ste. Madeleine."

Saint! What does this mean? And who is Madeleine? They must indeed worship these idols here. But this is wrong!

It was never the way of Yeshua!

She looked more closely at the lady Ste. Madeleine.
She may be a false idol, but they have made her very beautiful,
like a queen in golden gown and crimson cloak, she admitted,
smiling in her mind. But even thus gloriously robed, her face
is sad. People must see she is grieving. And for her to be
embracing that cross…!

Still bewildered and frustrated, she observed two men
joining the two women. The four of them stood together at
the foot of Ste. Madeleine's statue, gazing up at the figure,
seemingly lost in thought.

"Here she is again," said one of the women. "This is
her church. This is her center."

While watching the visitors point small black clicking
objects at the statue, she abruptly rose right through the
ceiling, soaring above the building, to view a countryside,
revealed in beauty beneath her.

Oh! Am I now an angel? She wondered incredulously.
Below, a familiar valley hemmed a high hill. There, above a
small village, stood the edifice she had just left. Flanking it
were two other buildings, a large house and a strange tower.

I know this place! she realized, although when I was
here before, there were no habitations on that height. I brought
baby Josephes with me while he was still a suckling at my
breast. We rested in a cave below the edge of this hill for
many days, teaching people who came to hear us from the
village below.

Instantly, in a flash, she found herself back in her body,
lying on the bed of furs.

Fully awakened now, she wondered at the purpose of
this vision. Could that magnificent church be the future of
Yeshua's Way?

It all seemed wrong; Yeshua taught surrounded by the
simplicity of fields, hills and deserts. How could his Way be
housed in such a glorious building? No, this could not be

Yeshua's house, although the truth might be hidden here. She did not understand.

In the future, she wondered, must truth be concealed from all but those who guard the secrets? She felt anger rise. Why should truth need to be concealed?

Whom will it serve to hide the truth?

* * * * *

By morning, the three red scratches had nearly disappeared. I showed them to Karol, who laughed, "You'd better be careful who you invite to visit during the night. There might be ghosts in a cottage this old!"

No explanation came to mind. Just a mystery, in a mysterious land. The Land of Oc. Curious name—reminds me of the land of Oz.

While Karol made coffee, I went outside on the patio, to pick some ripe figs for breakfast. In the north, a soft rainbow arced across a dewy cloud. What a lovely welcome to Languedoc! Oz, for sure. I snapped a picture. Omens are wonderful, at least the good ones.

We enjoyed doing some necessary laundry in a curious modern French washing machine that rested every few moments during its agitation cycle, while we enjoyed a leisurely lunch. Afterwards, Karol and I hiked up a rocky hill behind the old farmhouse.

Walking along Roman stone walled terraces, through Autumn's blazing vineyards, we arrived at a 12th Century church on the summit. It had been built to serve the ancient village of Siran, which is presently located lower, where there is more plentiful underground water.

The grapes had already been harvested, but we feasted on the gleanings, dark purple, sweet and seedy. My journal records our footsteps through the vineyards as accompanied by "munch, crunch, spit, swallow; munch, crunch, spit, swallow."

Waiting for the church to be opened for visitors was a pretty little 5-year-old girl, picking a bunch of tiny wildflowers.

Karol had found an abandoned bird's nest among the grapevines. She brought it to the child, who smiled delightedly, climbing up on a terrace to play with it. The bouquet, she told us in French I could easily understand, was for her mother, with whom she lived, in a house just out of sight beyond the church. Lucky mom, to have such a delightful child to bring such a sweet bouquet.

The Church of Our Lady of the Scintillating Aura (free translation) turned out to be well worth the wait. It is unique, because original, unrestored paintings decorate its interior walls. Romanesque in style, built of stone (as everything is in this part of France, because there is so much stone and so little wood available) its dim enclosure yielded a few surprises.

Surrounded by geometric designs, everybody seemed to be pictured on its walls— knights in armor, saints in processions, bishops, Saint Michael and the dragon, and a clutter of undecipherable figures, disfigured by the ravages of time.

In one area, a fascinating mural depicted a dark-skinned young woman, dressed in Egyptian style, a halo around her head. She stood above a crowd of people rendered in the traditional Egyptian way— body facing front, head in profile. Above the lady were some dark skinned, perplexing beings looking rather like monkeys with golden haloes, hanging from tree branches.

I called Karol over. "What do you make of this?" I asked.

"Don't know. Are those monkeys?"

"I'm not sure. Maybe they are saints hanging upside down, or climbing an arch to Heaven. In any case, look at the Egyptian influence here again, even if it's twelve centuries later. How odd that it persists so long."

"Reminds me of Sarah," she remarked, pointing to the dark skinned lady.

"Of course! This is another Black Madonna. There must be a story encoded in this mural! Perhaps it refers to Isis, the Egyptian Mother Goddess. People of the 12th century would have understood. Most of them could not read or write, so paintings and frescoes were their education."

Curiosity ruffled by the monkeys, we clambered back down the hill, stuffing our mouths with additional grapes on the return trip. Back at the cottage, we enjoyed a cup of tea on our flagstone patio, anticipating the imminent arrival of our colleagues. Sort of waiting for the opening curtain to rise, you might say.

Before the tea grew cold, a car drove up, disgorging Peter and Ross, waffle-legged and weary-bottomed from their long drive to join us.

Peter introduced his traveling companion Ross, a warm, teddy bear type of fellow. Italian by birth, Australian by adoption, Ross' geniality and kind heart transformed us from strangers to friends immediately.

Ross had joined Peter for one of his tours, deciding to travel with him further after the tour ended. Peter's tremendous knowledge and spirituality, and Ross' enthusiastic delight in just about everything, added new dimensions to our own journey.

We were all there to follow the Magdalene's footsteps wherever they might lead. Peter's awareness would help us understand how her presence in France fed into religions denounced by the Roman church. We were to come to look at "history" in a new light.

But for the moment, we needed to organize. Quickly deciding on how to divide up the chores, Ross and I agreed to take over the cooking, while Karol and Peter opted to do the cleaning up.

That suited Ross and me just fine. Pickup dinner that night was a feast of pasta with truffle sauce (Ross' delectable contribution from Italy), zucchini and cauliflower, salad, French bread dipped in olive oil and garlic, fruit, lemon yogurt and a delicious local white wine. Living proof was on our table that it's a fallacy vegetarian food is dull and tasteless!

After dinner, Peter cheerfully zipped into his mode as tour guide, lining up the next four days' itinerary. Early to bed, to arise at dawn and hit the road. Peter's an expert on shepherding groups of people, on time, to interesting places.

The following morning, after Ross had climbed the hill to watch the sunrise, and I had gathered breakfast figs and almonds from trees under a glorious pink dawn sky, (does this sound like Eden?) we embarked in a two-car caravan. Ross drove his Peugeot, Peter beside him navigating; Karol and I zooming after them in our little green Renault.

"Red sky in morning, sailors take warning," my Nova Scotia ancestors used to say. And they were right. By the time we arrived at the medieval town of Carcassonne, a misty rain was softly falling.

But that red sky held another little mystery. My photo, developed much later, showed a silvery disc among the clouds. Can't explain that either.

"Why don't we spend some time here in hopes the rain will taper off?" suggested Peter, disembarking from Ross' car in a parking lot near the gates to the medieval city. Agreeing, the four of us walked over a real drawbridge into a real walled city.

Despite the fact the drawbridge was also a road, so narrow one car could only pass at a time, the outside world ceased to exist the moment we moved through the huge wooden gates. Suddenly we were in the 13th century, a living museum—with modern amenities.

Drying off in a little café over hot chocolate and a *pain chocolat* (a flaky, melt in your mouth croissant pillow with a ribbon of chocolate in the middle— to die for—) we plotted the rest of the day.

Since rainy weather blots out good distance viewing, we decided to put off visiting hilltop Cathar castles for another excursion. Instead, we would tour Carcassonne, then travel on to Rennes-Le-Château, a hilltop village made famous in the book *Holy Blood, Holy Grail.*

Carcassonne, originally prehistoric, then Roman, Visigoth and Medieval French, was overtaken in the 13th Century Crusade against the Albigensians, and its outer walls destroyed. Rebuilt in the 19th Century, the city is perhaps the finest example of a fortified medieval town in the world. The city has 26 towers dotting its crenellated double walls. Within the inner fortifications are shops and cobbled streets, a cathedral, art galleries, and many restaurants.

We spent a couple hours browsing through this very interesting historic site, particularly enjoying an exhibition of marvelous photography of Cathar castles, and visiting the beautiful, ornate, Gothic Cathedral.

Eventually we left for our prime target of the day, Rennes-le-Château. The weather was clearing, so by the time we arrived at our destination, blue skies smiled and sun bathed the landscape in fresh brilliance.

Driving up the hill to Rennes-le-Château would scare the horns off a mountain goat. Karol's father used to compete in Vermont auto hill climbing races, and he had taught her a thing or two. She relished the challenge, accelerating around curves and hugging inside walls over steep drop-offs like a pro, while I just held onto my seat and closed my eyes.

But suddenly we were at the top, arriving at the end—a dirt parking lot on the doorstep of the Tour Magdala, the unique tower built next to the home of Abbé Saunière. Saunière was the priest who discovered some sort of mysterious treasure. The Tower was just a few doors away from the church he restored, using his sudden riches— the source of which has never been divulged.

Here we were! We had arrived right smack at the heart of an unsolved mystery!

"Howdja like that drive?" Ross called, alighting from his Peugeot.

"I did, I really did," rejoined Karol, much to Ross' surprise.

"Let's go right into the Church," suggested Peter. "They have a tour starting soon, and we don't want to miss it. We can

74

have lunch afterward."

"Right." We padded off to the church, known to contain the entire secret of Abbé Saunière within its walls. Waiting for the person in charge to open the doors, we read the mysterious sign over the doorway, *This Place is Terrible*, in Latin. A chilling welcome. Or perhaps it is better translated *This Place is Awesome,* for it certainly is.

Once inside, we were struck with the color and beauty of the place. Stepping past a hideous devil supporting the holy water basin, we turned to appreciate the four angels, each making a gesture of the sign of the cross, above it. They were equally as beautiful as he was grotesque.

"A remnant of the duality in Gnosticism," commented Peter. "The great tragedy of the Gnostics, which in part led to their downfall, was that they saw everything as either good or evil. They could not imagine God, who is good, could create evil— even though in the Old Testament, God created both. They were never able to connect the two as part of the Whole, which we now know to be the way things are. Good and evil are but two parts of the Whole; they are not separate from each other. Daylight and darkness are both parts of one day."

Beyond them was a large fresco of Jesus on a hill, preaching the Beatitudes to some people surrounding him. A woman with long red hair knelt in sorrow by his side.

"She's wearing the robes of Isis," I whispered to nobody in particular. We studied the painting. A branch bursting forth with flowers was in the lower right hand side, and a moneybag with a hole in it lay on the ground beneath the people's feet.

Karol stood beside me. "Could this bag of money refer to the treasure Mary and Joseph of Arimathea were supposed to have brought from the Temple in Jerusalem?" she asked in a low voice, looking around furtively. For some reason, it felt as if an unseen presence was with us.

"Could be," I answered. "This place is full of symbols and tricks. But in my opinion, the real treasure was the secret knowledge that Mary Magdalene and Jesus had children. The Church would need to suppress such information."

"There might be deeper meanings in these symbols as well," commented Karol. "Maybe connections to the Holy Grail." I nodded agreement.

We wandered around taking photographs. The blue, star-studded dome behind the altar gave colorful background to all the shots. And color was everywhere, even beaming through stained glass windows to anoint the statues. Saint Anthony stood on a pedestal in a place usually reserved for the Virgin Mary.

Why not? He is the patron saint of Lost Things, maybe even Found Treasures.

On the side of the pulpit, four Evangelists stood in a row, a canopy reminiscent of the Temple of Solomon above them. Behind the altar, a round stained glass window portrayed Mary Magdalene anointing the feet of Jesus. On the front of the altar, Mary Magdalene is painted kneeling tearfully before a cave, a skull by her knees, a budding cross and open book beside it. On the horizon of the background, appear what seems to be an Egyptian pyramid, and a gate to the city of Jerusalem. Did they signify the passage of hidden knowledge?

The kneeling figure is robed in gold, fingers clasped in a curious manner. Could it be a ritual handshake? Or some secret sign? The only warm, rosy colors are seen in her cheeks, and the front of her dress, which covers her lower abdomen. Abbé Saunière was supposed to have finished the details of the painting himself. What mysteries did he encode within it? Might the rosy abdomen signal a babe within her womb?

Eventually all four of us ended up at the feet of the statue of Ste. Madeleine. How beautiful this sad lady looked, in gold brocaded dress and crimson robe, clasped at the neck by a jewel. The Lady was supported on a cornice by two cherubic angels. In her hand she held the jar of precious spikenard used to anoint Jesus. The other arm held close a wooden cross, budding at the knotholes. By her feet, a skull rested upon an open book. We stood there, gazing up at her, for quite a long time.

"Here she is again," I said aloud. "This is her church. This is her center."

But If only you could speak to us! I mentally begged. *Dearest Mary of Magdala, here, we have found your image. Everything in this place is about you. You are in every echo, every beam of light. This is the secret of your universe, and we still don't understand.*

The Magdalene looked down at us unblinking. But it seemed to me, her sad face showed the very slightest hint of hope.

RENNES-LE-CHATEAU:
Statue of Mary Magdalene

Chapter Ten

RENNES-LE-CHATEAU

* * * * *

Dawn's first light dimmed the stars outside. How long she lay there, watching day slowly bring the cave's rocky walls into focus, she did not know. Her mind was still in that brightly painted church, sifting through new information about what the future might hold. It was too much, too unclear. Such a night of mysteries and marvels!

Shaking herself fully awake and present, she walked to the cavern's entrance. At the cliff's edge, she sank down upon her favorite meditation rock to watch the rising sun. Out across the valley below, light swept up in a golden wave, over the tops of trees, down into the hollows; finally penetrating the floor of the forest just below her perch and rising through the treetops to bathe her bare toes in its warmth.

Thus, the cycle of nature repeats itself, she observed. Dark and light give way to each other, day by day, season by season, year by year, aeon by aeon. Must not the cycles of civilizations rise and fall in harmony with the pattern? Must not the lives of humankind reflect a similar rhythm? Must we not be born, live, die and rise again?

Attracted by their cries, she watched ravens soaring above the trees on spiraling currents of wind.

"Yes! Like the flight of ravens," she mused aloud, aware of how aptly they illustrated the soaring thrust of her meditation.

Small sparrows fluttered upwards to sing joyous songs around her feet. Laughing delightedly, she ran back into the cave to fetch a crust of bread, left uneaten for days, which had been brought to her by faithful friend Maximim. She crumbled the bread, scattering it to the hungry birds, who pecked contentedly, making little chirping noises as they ate.

It was the hour of morning prayer. Warm in the early sunlight, she leaned back against the sheltering rock, closing her eyes. She imagined herself surrounded by angels, lifting her thoughts to the sky. All the mysteries of night dissolved into one glorious moment of union, communion with the Creator. Nourished, filled with light, she remained in ecstasy until a passing cloud cast its cool shadow across her face.

Arising languidly, she shook crumbs from her skirt and returned to bed.

"He is not yet through with me," she laughed aloud. "Tonight he will come again. But for a while, I shall sleep and dream. Quiet dreams. Restful dreams. Dreams of peace and beauty."

She closed her eyes, smiling sweetly.

"Au revoir, my love.

"Until we meet again tonight!"

* * * * *

Emerging from the church into bright daylight felt like splashing through a waterfall's cool shower, coming into an entirely different landscape on the other side. One experiences similar sharp contrasts upon returning to ordinary life from any sacred space, whether it be church, sweat lodge, concert, theatre or any other environment where present day reality is suspended temporarily, allowing communion, imagination and emotion freedom to reign.

And, just as suddenly, my stomach reminded me of lunch not yet eaten.

I steered the others to the only restaurant open at that off-season time of year, perched on the edge of the cliff right beside

Abbé Saunière's garden. What a view! Sitting at a table beside the window, we took turns observing the countryside below. In the distance, snow-capped Pyrenees Mountains hung on the horizon, green foothills hugging their skirts. Nestled in the valley directly below, like a hen setting on her nest, a town settled itself on the banks of a river flanked by fertile fields patched in varying harvest hues.

"This must have been an important strategic point," observed Ross, the engineer, looking out over the landscape.

"It was indeed," responded Peter, the historian. "The Visigoths, after pillaging Rome and taking possession of the colossal treasure of Jerusalem, which had been brought to Rome in 10 AD, occupied the whole south of France and Spain. With nearby Toulouse as their capital, they created the most powerful and brilliant kingdom of the entire western world."

"Ah, yes, were they Christians?"

"Visigoths became Christians, and were highly skilled builders. Right here on this hill they created the town of Rhedae, constructing a complete stronghold, a powerful fortress flanked by two citadels and encircled by a double set of ramparts. In the 8th Century Rhedae was considered the equal of Narbonne and Carcassonne. It was rumored the entire treasure of Jerusalem was secreted here."

"But how did this big town become the little village we see today?" Karol wondered aloud, breaking off a piece of bread and passing the loaf to Ross.

In response to her question, Peter continued his discourse. "In 1209, under cover of fighting the Cathar heresy, the town was destroyed by the infamous Simon de Montfort and his Crusaders. He had been sent by King Philippe Auguste of France to subdue Languedoc and restore the lands to dominion by the French Crown. Although it was subsequently partially rebuilt, bandits and warring soldiers of fortune razed the fortifications and destroyed the church. What they did not destroy, the Plague did. The town never fully recovered."

"And the treasure of the Visigoths?"

"Some say this is what made good Abbé Saunière suddenly rich."

"So what is the real story of the mystery here?" Ross asked, between mouthfuls of crisp *frites*. (They're not called *French* fries for nothing!) And Ross does love his frites!

Having wolfed down my sandwich, I decided to give Peter a chance to eat his lunch. "OK, I'll be the story teller," I volunteered cheerfully. "I just finished reading the guidebook while we were in the car."

"In 1886 the Abbé Béranger Saunière began restoration of what was then the chapel of Sainte Madeleine, using funds donated by an emissary of Countess de Chambord, whose dead husband had been a pretender to the throne of France. Under this arrangement, the Abbé was to look for any precious documents that were reported to be hidden in the church, and turn over any he found to the Countess.

"There had been a great secret passed down in the family of the Marquise d'Hautpoul de Blanchefort, who had owned Rennes-le-Château. When she was about to die, she passed the secret and some important documents on to her parish priest Abbé Antoine Bigou, the predecessor by 100 years of Abbé Saunière. Bigou hid the documents in the Visigoth pillar that held up the altar in the Sainte Madeleine church. This was just before the French Revolution of 1789, which was about to put the nation in turmoil, and even threatened his own life."

"Yes, those were perilous times," agreed Karol, using the leftover bread to mop up olive oil stranded on her plate.

"Right. Not only did he hide the documents, but also he added two others, which contained coded messages." I consulted the book, which I had pulled from my backpack.

"One translated to 'SHEPHERDESS, NO TEMPTATION THAT POUSSIN TENIERS HOLD THE KEY; PEACE 681 BY THE CROSS AND THIS HORSE OF GOD I

COMPLETE (OR DESTROY) THIS DAEMON OF THE GUARDIAN AT NOON BLUE APPLES.'"

"Huh?" from Ross.

"The other coded parchment was no less confusing. It read 'TO DAGOBERT II AND TO SION BELONGS THIS TREASURE AND HE IS THERE DEAD.'

"Bigou also did some other odd things. He had a flat tombstone brought from the 'Tomb of Arques,' a small funeral monument situated on the French 0 Meridian nearby, to place on the grave of the late Marquise in the churchyard. Into the Latin inscription thereon, which read 'ET IN ARCADIA EGO,' and the epitaph of the Marquise, he encoded the same information."

"He went to a lot of trouble," Karol remarked, laying down her napkin.

"It must have been something fantastic to be worth that much effort," added Ross.

"Well I think the Abbé Bigou felt he was safeguarding the secrets for posterity," I continued. "You know, it was very fashionable in those times to dabble in secret languages and ciphers. But before he died, Bigou passed the secrets along to two other men, Abbé Jean Vié, parish priest of Rennes-les-Bains from 1840-1870; and Abbé Émile Francois Cayron, parish priest of St. Laurent de la Cabrerisse in the Aude district, at the same period of time.

"Almost a hundred years later, in 1886, Saunière began to restore the church, and in that same year a priest trained by Abbé Cayron wrote a peculiar book. His name was Abbé Boudet, and the book's title translates to *The True Celtic Language and the Stone Circle of Rennes-les-Bains*. In the book he conceals, between the lines, the mysterious secret of the Hautpol de Blanchefort, and gives the exact location of 12 chests, each of which can be opened with a special number. The book was not well received, so he decided to encode the same information in the decorations of the church, which Saunière was restoring.

"It was also in that same year Saunière discovered parchments in a stone altar support. He took the papers

83

immediately to Paris, to the Church of St. Sulpice. Whatever the papers were, they seem to have given him ingress into high Parisian society and esoteric circles."

We had all finished eating and had pushed away our plates to continue discussing the story.

"Has anyone figured out what the blue apples message meant?" asked Ross leaning back in his chair.

"It seems to refer to the Church of St. Sulpice, in Paris," answered Peter. That church is an esoteric temple, copied from the Temple of Solomon, and finished at the time of the Marquise de Blanchefort's death. It stands on the territory of the Abbey of St. Germain des Près, where the Merovingian kings were buried at that time. It tells whoever understands the message to remain silent until the year 1891."

"Why 1891? In the inscription it says 681."

"Because the epitaph on the Marquise's tomb shows that date. It should have read 17 January, 1781, in Roman letters, (XVII Janvier MDCCLXXI) but Bigou added a 0, which doesn't exist in Roman numerals, to replace the second C; which in effect subtracts a century, causing it to read 1681. And if you use that 0 (which is the old French meridian on which both St. Sulpice and Rennes-les-Bains are located) as a pivot to turn the numerals 1681 upside down, you get 1891."

"Clever! But what significance does 1891 have?"

"It is the very year Abbé Saunière made his famous discovery."

"Wow, what a story," Ross sighed, appetite apparently satisfied by the excellent *frites*. "But just exactly what did Abbé Saunière discover?"

"He found a tomb under a stone that had been turned face down by Bigou just before he left town 100 years earlier. Steps led down to a vault in which there seems to have been some gold and skeletons. Some say a special skull. But whatever he found there, from that day on, the Abbé and his housekeeper Marie Denaraud were rich people."

"But the blue apples?" Ross persisted.

"In the winter, the sun's rays focus through a blue colored stained glass window at the south end of the church, turning blue some round fruit in a painting of a tree on the opposite wall. At noon. Just three of them. The rest are red. The same phenomenon used to occur in the Church of St. Sulpice, but it disappeared in 1891 to appear at Rennes-le-Château instead."

Four sets of raised eyebrows reflected the weirdness of so much coincidence.

"That's only one of the mysteries hidden in the church we just visited," Peter added, breaking the silence. "People come from all over to try to figure them out. Information is coded into the Stations of the Cross, the paintings, even the black and white chessboard floor—and who knows what else? It has become the newest esoteric gathering place. Over 25,000 people visit it each year. Abbé Saunière's house is now a bed and breakfast, housing tourists on the upper floors."

"Didn't the artist Poussin paint a picture of the tomb near Arques, where the flat stone came from?" asked Karol.

"Yes, and so many people have gone to see it, that the man who owns the property where it was located became forced to demolish the tomb. It was one point of a sacred landscape temple in the shape of a pentagram."

A waitress came over with the bill. It was time to go outside and see for ourselves just what the riches of Abbé Saunière had accomplished.

"There is a connection here with the Knights Templar as well," said Peter as we were paying the check and exiting the restaurant. "Another great heresy, another great mystery. Did you notice the skull and crossbones on the arch at the entrance to the cemetery by the church? A Templar symbol. Le Bézu, that citadel to the south, was a Templar stronghold. One of the Grand Masters was a Blanchefort. The Blanchefort Castle lies to the northeast. They act as two protective fortresses for Rennes-le-Château.

"The Cathars connect to this place too. This is an area of great sacred mystery. You know that inscription over the door of the Church, which translates 'This place is terrible'? It can also be translated 'This place is awesome.' And the rest of the quotation is completed on the arch of the porch. It reads 'It is the House of God and the Gate of Heaven.' The quotation is from the Book of Genesis, Chapter 28, Verse 17."

"Peter, will you tell us more about the Templars and the Cathars?"

"Of course," he smiled, "but over a glass of wine in our kitchen at LeThéron, Does that sound OK?"

Natch. So, putting those mysteries on hold, we explored Abbé Saunière's domain, mysteries enough for the moment. Walking up the street from the church, we began our tour at the southernmost part of his establishment, the Tour Magdala, (Magdalene Tower), which had greeted us, dominating the parking lot. Built at the beginning of the 20th century, the Tower possesses a medieval majesty out of character with France of the modern era. It perches on the edge of the cliff, which falls away nearly a thousand feet to the valley below.

The tower, built of stone, with a crenellated watchtower of 12 crenels (the same number as signs of the zodiac) was originally named the Clocktower. Its orientation gave it usefulness as a sundial. Abbé Saunière built the Tour Magdala on two levels, plus the tower itself. Those two levels were to serve as his private study and library.

More mystery: not far from the tower, between fallen rocks and the cliff, diggers discovered a prehistoric shelter under the rocks, filled with bones of women and children. It is also said that there is an underground passage which runs along a natural rift in the rock, leading from the Tower to the aforementioned Castle of Blanchefort, which stood guard over the valley of Rennes-les-Bains until it was destroyed, along with Rennes-le-Château, by Simon de Montfort.

Leading north from the Tower, along the edge of the cliff, is a curved walkway, serving as a rampart, at the other end of which stands a glass greenhouse. We proceeded over to the greenhouse, now missing most of its glass and in a state of disrepair. Nevertheless, Karol discovered some fresh parsley still growing inside. A remnant of the Past, blooming on into the Present!

It was easy to imagine how the place must have looked around 1900, as the good Abbé and his Marie entertained the cream of Paris society in gardens encircled by the walkway and spilling over in front of his mansion, the Villa Bethania. Their guests were prominent in esoteric and occult *salons* much in vogue at that time among such Parisian intellectuals. One famous occultist, opera singer Emma Calvé, was a frequent guest, and rumored to be Saunière's lover. Interestingly, a relative of hers, Mélanie Calvet (Calvé's surname before she changed the spelling) was one of two children who saw visions of the Virgin Mary at La Salette in the French Alps. Later in life, Mélanie became a mystic, censured by the Roman Catholic Church for her "salacious" writings. There seems to have been an undercurrent of sacred sexuality running through the belief systems of these occultists and through the mystery of Rennes-le-Château. Sacred marriage? Mary and Jesus? Temple virgins? We really do not know.

Saunière's home, Villa Bethania, (named after Bethany, town where Mary and Martha entertained Jesus) has two ground rooms open to public viewing. The living room, wallpapered in expensive fabric, and lavishly appointed in the style of the day, leads to a dining room, also beautifully furnished. On a white linen tablecloth rests a bottle of Rennes-le-Château wine, grown and bottled on Village estates. A photograph of Saunière is placed on an antique sideboard. His strong, chiseled countenance gives no hint of the mysteries perpetrated in this awesome place.

Turning to exit through the living room, I noticed a particularly beautiful gilt framed mirror above the fireplace, reflecting a Chinese, lantern-style light fixture hanging from the ceiling in the center of the room. Positioned on chests and tables were porcelain figures, and a statue of the Infant of Prague given to him by the Sisters of the Sacred Heart in Paris for his mysterious "service to our kind King."

He had eclectic taste, this man, and apparently the money to indulge it.

The door led out to a beautiful solarium, roofed with panes of colored glass. As with the greenhouse, most were broken; yet the sun still bathed a large figure of Christ on the Cross, dominating the solarium, in magenta and amber light. How glorious it must have been when new!

Outside, in the garden, a life sized bronze statue of a weeping woman knelt within a stone circle. Was this another reference to the Magdalene?

We spent quite a bit of time in the museum by the Church, and the smaller museum on the lower level of the Tour Magdala. There, we viewed extensive documents and photographs relating to Abbé Saunière and Marie Denarnaud, their life in Rennes-le-Château, the restoration of the Church, building of his personal domain, his wealth and eventual bankruptcy. This has all occurred since the advent of cameras; therefore documenting the story with a precision not available until recently. (Saunière died in 1917, and Marie Denarnaud lived until 1953.) Nothing in those annals seemed very mysterious, yet an elusive feeling of enigma continues to saturate the atmosphere, coloring our emotions with a veil of smoky lavender-gray.

Why has the "secret" never been divulged? After Saunière's death, Marie promised Noël Corbu, who bought the Villa Bethania, that she would tell him the secret before she died. Unfortunately she became senile before her death from a stroke, and never was able to relate it. So the mystery remains.

As I exited the lower museum, I noticed someone had placed a large poster in a sequestered alcove below the Tower. It stopped me in my tracks.

"Guys, come here," I called to the others disappearing down some steps. They returned, alerted by my tone of voice.

We crowded around, examining the poster.

In somber colors of blue and rose, the Tour Magdala was painted against a dark sky, with a crescent moon, stars, and clouds forming fantastic figures behind the Tower, and two pine trees in silhouette. In this poster, a circular staircase led from below the Tower, underground, to a cave in which lay a wooden chest. A wraithlike woman in black stood upon the stairs, leading forth from the cavern an apparently dead man. Where their hands touched, light glowed, reminding us of God touching Adam on the Sistine Chapel ceiling. It was surreal, it was eerie, and it was breathtaking. Below the image was a reproduction of the equal-armed Templar Cross, the word MAGDALA in Gothic letters, and the town's name, Rennes-le-Château.

We looked at the poster, almost expecting the earth to open and that specter to emerge at our feet, until the hair began to rise on the back of our necks.

"Time to get out of here," Ross whispered.

"Right," said Peter.

"Yep," agreed Karol.

"Uh-huh," I muttered.

We retreated in a hurry.

Looking over our shoulders, as if the woman in black were following, we made a beeline for the ordinary safety of the parking lot.

How were we to know then, our days together in Languedoc would produce even more mysteries and strange experiences?

It's like the old saying: "When the student is ready, the teacher appears."

I guess we must have been ready, because the teachers were lining up to get our attention.

And they did.

RENNES-LE-CHATEAU:
Poster Near the Tour Magdala

Chapter Eleven

ROOTS OF THE CATHARS

* * * * *

Afternoon light startled her to consciousness. Had she slept until morning? Had he not come as promised? She rubbed her eyes, peering at the bright sky outside her cave. The sun was just past the zenith. With great relief, she realized she had rested only a few hours.

Approaching footsteps intruded upon the silence of her hermitage. Who could it be? Her visitors were few, only old friends Maximim; occasionally Lazarus and Sarah. Helena and Jacoba had gone to heaven long since. Occasionally her children; Tamar, Josephes, and Yeshua the Younger— whom they now called Justus— came to see to her welfare, but they too were getting older, and busy with their own lives. Those visits were few, and far between.

It could not be her brother-in-law James, the Joseph of Arimathea, for he was making one of his periodic journeys to trade for tin, in the islands far to the north.

Ah, yes, what was she thinking? It was probably dear cheerful Maximim, climbing up on one of his regular trips to bring her provisions.

Hastening to the opening of her cave, she observed a man dressed in brown, leading a donkey of matching color, carefully making his way up the steep path through the forest. As they came into view, she recognized the visitor.

"James! Dear James!" she called. "Come hence, dear brother-in-law. You are most welcome!"

91

The man and beast lumbered up the rocky last few steps onto the ledge. He led the donkey into the shelter of the cave, where the animal stood still, breathing heavily under his load of mysterious bundles.

"Sister, I salute you." James, the Joseph of Arimathea, knelt to kiss her hand.

"Nay, James, you need not treat me as a queen." She blushed a little, brushing back her hair in absentminded habit. "Do come rest from your arduous climb. Pray take some water." She ladled a dipper of water from the cistern, holding it towards him. Gratefully, the old man drank deeply. Returning the dipper to the source, she scooped water into a wooden bowl, placing it on the floor for the donkey to drink.

"You arrive unexpectedly," she remarked. "The more your welcome."

"Thank you, dear sister. I have brought food and drink, so you may break your needless fast and celebrate my safe return from Britannia. The road becomes more dangerous every year, and I am tired of traveling. This has been my last journey."

"You will travel no more, then?"

"As I said— and we shall drink to that!"

A new sound— her merry laughter— echoed from the cavern walls.

How it pleased him to see her happy again! Riding on the sound of that laughter, the beautiful young priestess of memory returned to fill his heart once more.

She watched him unload some packages from the patient donkey's back. How he creates joy! she thought. In many ways he is different from his brother Yeshua. It is true that James is stricter in his observation of the Law, and now that he shepherds the Movement created by Yeshua, many people judge him to be stern— yet as a friend, there is a sparkle in his eye, warmth in his heart, and merriment in his manner.

Perhaps I have forgotten the happiness of human companionship in my retreat from the world. How strange, to thus retrieve it, when I feel about to leave this life behind forever!

Spreading a cloth upon the floor, the Joseph placed wondrous fare upon it—bread, cheese, fresh fruit, dried fruit, and a skin of wine. He untied the skin's neck, looking about for a vessel to hold the wine for drinking.

"I have but one container, the dipper from which you drank." She was suddenly embarrassed at her lack of amenities.

"No matter, we shall share it. We can pass it from one to the other like the wedding cup. We shall celebrate together the memory of my brother." He offered the dipper to her. The wine tasted sweet and heady, opening her heart.

"I have seen Yeshua" she confided.

Startled, he looked long in her eyes, then drank a draught of wine before responding. "In what manner, sweet sister? Has he returned in his body as before?"

"I do not think so. It is more like a vision, yet I hear him clearly and he is showing me many mysteries."

"Mysteries?"

"Ah yes, to the point I question my own perceptions."

"Dear Sister, take and eat of this food, and tell me all."

He listened attentively as she related what had happened the past night. When she had finished the telling, he took another sip of wine, wiped his mouth on his sleeve, and looked her full in the eyes.

"He is preparing you," he said, taking her hand in comfort.

"I do believe that," she sighed, "but for what? I wish it were easier to understand."

She brightened. "But where are my manners? I have ignored my guest. Pray tell me of your journey as the official

93

tin procurer of Rome."

"As usual," he replied. "Sore muscles, lack of sleep, mosquitoes, snakes, attacks by bandits, hard luck, little profit...."

"It is small wonder you retire from that travail." Removing her hand from his, she sipped again from the dipper, smiling. "It is our good fortune to have you safely home for good."

Falling into deep thought, he absently offered her some figs, which she politely declined. "Perhaps it is better, seeing how my brother is revealing hidden knowledge to you, to remind you of one small piece of the puzzle. You can judge for yourself how it fits into the whole."

"Of what do you speak?"

"Of that journey to the Northern Isles when we built the church in your name."

"My name?"

"You did not know that?"

"Nay, and I am humbled before it."

He took her hand again, earnestly relating the story of how he brought twelve of their friends, Yeshua's disciples, and her own small son Yeshua the younger, to the sacred place in Britannia, beside the river leading to the sea.

He described in detail, to refresh her memory, how the king of that northern place had traded land for twelve hides, receiving the men warmly, as if aware of their holy mission. He recalled planting his staff, a branch of the thorn tree of Jerusalem, and how it flowered, signifying the Word had been planted in this foreign land. James, the Joseph spoke of placing a cup in a holy well, confirming that the Holy Grail, the Mystery of Understanding, had been symbolically concealed there; and he told of building a little church of branches and mud, for worshiping the Truth Yeshua taught.

"And I called it the church of Mary, to honor the sacred Feminine Mystery, and also to honor you, who carried forth *the blood of our Master. Young Yeshua sanctified it himself, with water mixed from the red well and the white well, signifying sacred marriage of the male and female, heaven and earth."*

As his words faded away, she bowed her head and kissed the hem of his robe, grateful for hearing how Yeshua's Word had spread to the North, and been established in a church bearing her own name, and that of the Mother of the Man.

Tears of wonder and joy moistened the dusty brown fabric, just as her tears had once anointed the dusty feet of her beloved.

* * * * *

Barreling back down the mountain, Karol proved once again she would be capable of competing in the *Grand Prix*. As for me, white knuckles from grasping the dashboard were the only outward sign of terror. I was not about to distract her by fruitless screaming.

Once safely down the hill and onto the flats, we followed Ross and Peter into the nearby old Roman spa town of Rennes-les-Bains. Peter had visited it previously, and there was a little church he wanted to see again. He said it had good energy.

Rennes-les-Bains rambles along both sides of a rushing river bordered by high cliffs. Named for old Roman thermal baths— which we, however, did not see— its history reaches much further back into tribal times.

Certainly another sacred place, it, too, figured in the mystery of Rennes-le-Château. It was Abbé Jean Vié of Rennes-les-Bains, who was one of the two priests entrusted with the "secret" by a fleeing Abbé Bigou in 1792, a hundred years before Abbé Saunière discovered the "treasure."

However, it was another kind of mystery that awaited us in the entry room of the church— an iron crucifix with a Madonna and Child in its center.

Karol was the first to spot it. "Look at this, Cinnie," she whispered. Instead of Jesus hanging on the cross, a black iron Madonna holding a black iron Infant in the center of a black iron Crucifix smiled back at us. Moreover, the cross was decorated with leafy vines bearing roses. A pleasant contrast to the usual gruesome, dead Jesus crucifix.

"I never saw anything like this before," I exclaimed excitedly, drawing the attention of Peter and Ross. Apparently, none of us had, judging by raised shoulders and shaking heads. No answers, only silent questions filled the space between us.

Inside the church, glowing light streamed through a stained glass window, illuminating a statue of Jesus of the Sacred Heart. It stood above an altar adorned with two golden candlesticks flanking a more traditional crucifix. Light, in rainbow colors, cascaded down the wall, flowing over the figures, puddling on the altar's spotless white linen cloth.

After pausing for a few moments of prayer, our group of four passed through a side entrance into the cemetery, where we meandered about among many family tombs, covered in local style by slabs of beautiful granite and marble. Decorated with statues, angels, and baskets of flowers, each hallowed enclosure contained many generations, resting just a few feet above the joyfully burbling river.

"Hey, guys," I called softly, so as not to disturb some other visitors to the cemetery. "Come here. There's another one." We gathered around a rusting, iron crucifix adorning an old grave, to marvel at another Madonna and Child placed in its center. This one had stars bursting forth from the corners of the cross.

Ross, ever ready to shoot, aimed his camera for a close-up. "Why do you suppose she is being honored above Jesus here?" he wondered aloud, adjusting the focus. "At least it seems like she is."

"It would be appropriate, if this area is indeed a center of the Magdalenian cult," I surmised. "Especially if people know her as the representation of earlier Isis worship. Remember, Isis is usually shown with infant Horus in her arms."

"Right," joined in Peter, "it may be a strand of the earlier belief systems showing up again in a new culture. A secret 'knowing' by the people who lived here."

"But it is odd," Karol commented, "to see a woman on the cross. Don't you find it unsettling?"

"Absolutely." We turned to leave the graveyard, exiting through the church once again. Walking through the vestibule, I said a little prayer to the Madonna on the cross and gently patted her shoulder. The metal felt warm to my touch.

On the way back to our cottage, we stopped to buy groceries, which transformed into yet another gourmet vegetarian dinner, consisting this time of couscous, wild mushrooms, local broccoli—and of course, local wine to accompany it.

After Karol and Peter had tidied up the kitchen, we took our half-empty glasses into our cozy little den, to hear Peter tell us about the Cathars, as he had promised.

"To understand the Cathars, you have to go way back in history," he began. We settled comfortably in the couches, listening attentively.

"Probably it should start with the beginnings of humankind, but we don't have much written history before the Sumerians. Certainly as long as there have been people, there have been religions. Most likely, original religion was worshiping forces of nature and a creator Goddess, symbol of that great mystery peculiar to women, the ability to give birth. Fertility.

"All religion centered around some form of Deity providing for people. Fertility of the earth and creatures upon the earth depended upon these gods, and the survival of mankind depended upon them too. This theme of fertility has pervaded all religion up to and including present days. We just became more sophisticated. We think we can control everything."

"Technology," offered Ross. Didn't the Atlanteans make the same mistake?"

"So they say," added Karol, "but I'll bet that's another story."

"Right," Peter smiled. "But I might add, fertility is the recurrent theme in Grail legends too—a wounded king whose lands are barren until the Grail, (always carried by a woman, by the way,) is found and restores the king to health. Then the land becomes fertile once more. The king is always wounded in the groin, so you can guess where that symbolism is going."

"Sex?" asked Ross, hopefully.

"Into the concept of sacred marriage?" I guessed.

"You're right," Peter confirmed, "but that too is a whole other story, best kept for another evening."

We sighed, a little disappointed.

Peter continued as if he didn't notice. "All through the evolution of cultures, Gods and Goddesses have personified archetypal qualities, which governed the well-being of humans. At the same time, human psychological qualities such as anger, jealousy, love and hatred were projected upon the Gods by people unaware of the true nature of their own relationship with the Cosmos.

"Storms, earthquakes, droughts and floods were some of the natural forces controlled by these deities. So, you see, humans thought that by pleasing the Gods and Goddesses they could control them."

"Control their world, right?" echoed Karol, gesturing towards Ross with her empty glass.

"Right. They used rituals to impress the divinities. We might call it magic."

"Hold it, until I get back!" Ross scurried to the kitchen to bring another bottle of wine. It gave me a moment to make some notes in my journal. *Magic...three Wise Men... Magi... magicians?*

"OK, mates," Ross said, returning; only with his Australian accent it sounded more like "mites".

"Just a mite more," I punned, holding out my glass.

98

Ross, always affable, laughed and filled it. Peter and Karol groaned.

"Are we ready?" Peter was in a bit of a hurry to get on with his lecture. A tour guide has to know a lot, educate a lot, be his delightful self— and get some sleep too. (Even when travelling with occasionally rowdy friends like us.) He held out his glass for a refill too.

"Let's see.… Settle down, this is serious stuff. Here these people of old were trying to control the universe with their rituals. And human nature being what it is, they soon began controlling other people too."

We did settle down, listening carefully.

"Mystery schools developed. One example is the Eleusinian Mysteries of Greece, which ritualized the mysterious cycles of winter, spring, and summer; death and rebirth; embodied in the myth of Demeter and Persephone.

"These mystery schools consisted of various cults in which secret knowledge was restricted to inner circles, the initiates. Even within the initiates there were inner circles, the elite. The elite got to know the super-secret mysteries. See the pattern here?"

"Reminds me of some of the secret brotherhoods today— Freemasons, Rosicrucians, Knights Templar…"

Peter interrupted my recitation of the list. "Right. The same. You see, although these secret societies exist today, their beginnings are lost in the misty dawn of humanity. Their family trees are rooted in the soil of Mesopotamia's fertile crescent."

I made another note: *the sacred spiral…same stuff, new cultures…*

"Well," Peter continued, "somewhere back then people began to try to figure out why there were bad things and good things—why people did evil deeds, while at other times they did loving ones—why a deity who brought sun and rain also brought hail and locusts to destroy the crops—why there was sickness and death in the same world with beauty and life. And so on.

"It was pretty easy to assign these things to different Gods and Goddesses. But what happens when you come to believe there is only one God?" Peter looked around at each of us, eyebrows raised, enjoying the quiz.

I actually raised my hand. "You have to invent the devil!" I blurted.

Everyone laughed. I blushed, feeling like a schoolgirl.

"They may not have called it the devil, but you're right, Cynthia. Someone had to be the bad guy, responsible for all the woes in life. And someone had to be the good guy." He waved his glass in an emphatic arc. "So developed *duality,* the polarity between good and evil.

"One of the first monotheistic (one god) and therefore dualistic (good and evil) religions was Zoroastrianism, which emerged thousands of years before Christianity. Maybe as long before as 6,000 BCE."

"What does BCE mean?" Karol asked. "I think I know, but can't quite remember the words."

"Before the Common Era. BCE and CE are now more often used than BC and AD. After all, most of the world is not Christian, so why use 'Before Christ' and 'The Year of Our Lord' in a world which is now so intimately interconnected?"

Karol nodded agreement. "That's what I thought. So go ahead and tell us. What was Zoroastrianism about?"

"It was named after its Persian founder Zoroaster. He preached that there was only one god, named Ahura Mazda, who is supreme. But evil was personified in a spirit of violence and death called Angra Mainyu."

"Angry Man, You?" from Ross. (Laughter.)

"Who knows? Perhaps that's where the word 'anger' really did come from. But listen to this, my friends: According to Zoroaster:

—mankind must choose whether to follow evil or good,
—evil will be destroyed at the end of time,
—at death the soul is judged and goes to heaven or hell,

100

—and a savior will be born of a virgin. This savior will raise the dead and judge everyone in a final judgement. Sound familiar?"

It was sort of shocking. *Wow. That Spiral again. I wonder how many times it has come around?*

"You said?" Peter was looking at me. I must have been thinking aloud. "I was just wondering how many times those concepts have come back again in different time frames and different cultures."

"A lot. While we're on the subject, here's another one for you to wonder about. In Arabia, around 400 BCE, there was a religion headed by a prophet named 'Issa,' which translates into Iesous in Greek, and Jesus in Aramaic. This Issa had a virgin mother named Mary. And he was crucified, resurrected and ascended into heaven. Familiar, again? You can still recognize these themes in modern Christian religion."

"Touché," Karol agreed. "But how does this relate to the Cathars?"

"The concept of dualism continued down through the years and cultures. It moved through Egypt, through offshoots of the Hebrew religion, and through a parallel religion called *Gnosticism,* which probably also descended from Zoroastrianism.

"When Jesus sought to update the Jewish religion, he was also operating in the basically dualist manner of using Satan to personify evil. But he was also challenging Jewish structure, by teaching a very Gnostic belief—that it was not necessary to have intermediary priests and high priests; because one can communicate directly with God. This probably got him in a lot of trouble with the orthodox Jews."

"Religion is Politics," I offered. "I read that somewhere."
"True. One need only to look at the history of Northern Ireland to see it still is— but back to the connections with the Cathars:"

"OK."

"When Jesus was crucified, his teachings continued on in two directions. In one stream, Peter and Paul established the Roman church, based on succession by the apostles. In the other

101

stream, his teachings went to France with Mary Magdalene and her companions, where they continued in religions soon branded 'Heretic' by the Roman Christian church.

"Once established in France, they diffused and expanded into a number of other sects. The Culdeans were the earliest Christians in England, established by Joseph of Arimathea and a group of disciples, who brought the 'Holy Grail' to Britian around 40-45 CE.

"Some other important groups in the Magdalenean stream over the first twelve centuries were the Manicheans, Marcionites, Massalians, Paulicans and most lately the Bogomils, who developed in the Balkan area. From the Bogomils a number of splinter groups broke off, among them the Cathars."

"That was a whole bunch of religions. What did they have in common, that Rome denounced them?"

"First of all, they threatened the power of the dominant church, the orthodox Roman church, by claiming no need for hierarchy, since they had direct communication with the Creator. This means they did not have to obey the Pope and bishops.

"Also, these religions believed they could achieve salvation, not through Jesus' sacrifice, but through *gnosis*, or personal knowledge. Thirdly, they believed in the equality of all people, and that included women. A secret tradition honoring women, which was a remnant of the Goddess worship of pagan times, was carried on through them. This is the underground stream in which Mary Magdalene became representative of the Goddess."

It was getting late, the wine was gone, and Peter had given us a lot of information.

Exhausted from the day's adventures, we were ready for sleep, even though we had yet to learn all we would have liked to have known about the Cathars.

"Why don't we go in one car tomorrow?" suggested Ross. "Then Peter can tell us more about the Cathars while we are driving to Minerve."

"Good idea," Peter responded, and we all agreed. "We'll need to start early."

Nearly overwhelmed with the sights, insights, sounds, tastes, smells and mysteries of the day, we four weary adventurers climbed the worn stone steps to sleep and dream of ancient Gods and Goddesses, forces of good and evil, and buried treasure.

Enough for one day! Tomorrow, we suspected, would be even more full of interesting events. And so it was.

RENNES-LE-CHATEAU:
Cynthia at the Tour Magdala

RENNES-LE-CHATEAU:
Abbé Saunière's House

RENNES-LE-CHATEAU:
Abbé Saunièr's Parlor

Chapter Twelve

MINERVE

* * * * *

In silence, James, the Joseph lifted her head from the hem of his garment, wiping tears from her eyes with his sleeve. He held her frail, light body close to his chest, stroking her tousled hair as a father would console a small child.

"There, now, dear sister, you have humbled yourself too much. Shall I tell you a story? The evening is not yet upon us." Yes, it would be comforting, she thought. She drew back nodding, a smile returning to brighten her tear stained face.

"I know... I shall tell you a creation story, one quite unlike that in the Torah. Some of it will feel familiar to you, for it rubs shoulders with our own beliefs"

"Pray do tell me, kind brother James."

"As you wish." He rose slowly to his feet, rubbing one hip into life again. The old man became actor as well as storyteller.

"In the beginning," his voice increased in volume with the gesture of his arm towards Heaven, "there was True God alone. He was the Monad. True God always existed, and always will. Infinite and unknowable."

She bobbed her head in acknowledgement, settling more comfortably onto her bed to hear.

"True God was lonely. He was named Depth." The actor's hand descended towards the floor of the cave.

"So he created a female counterpart, Silence." The hand moved over the old man's mouth, forefinger raised. "Together they created fourteen pairs of Aeons, divine emanations." He continued his pantomime, arms waving, matching actions to words.

She sat, raptly listening.

"The Aeons were descending levels of awareness and power, and at the bottom was the partnership of the Creator God, and Sophia, that is to say Wisdom.

"But Sophia was not always wise. Somewhere along the way, without the knowledge of her consort, she created another God who was known by several names: Yaldabaoth, Samael and Saclas. This God's wisdom was less than his power, which is why the meanings of his names are 'Child of the Chaos,' 'Blind God,' and 'Foolish One.'"

"This is the God of the Torah?"

"Yes, sister. But in that he is known as Yahweh, or Jehovah. He is the God who created the world, and First Man and First Woman.

"Sophia did not find the result of his creations satisfactory, so she infused her spark of wisdom into them. Therefore Yahweh was only half a creator, and Sophia is also our divine mother." His arms described two circles in the air, intersecting each other.

First Man, Adam, was the embodiment of Soul; whilst First Woman, Eve, was the incarnation of Spirit. Soul contains the thinking part of personality, the Lesser Self. Spirit is transcendental, the Higher Self. Therefore, Eve was superior, not inferior, to Adam. It is she who is the giver of life. That is why Sophia's mystical name is Zoe, which means Life."

The woman, excited, could not refrain from interrupting his tale. "This is why the Master taught that women must not be considered inferior!"

"Quite so," affirmed the Joseph. He paused for a moment, regaining his train of thought, body rocking slightly

108

to and fro as if to stimulate the mind.

"Adam fell into a deep sleep, claims the Torah. I would say what it means is he was not actually sleeping, but unconscious of himself. It was Eve, emerging through Adam's state of unconsciousness, who gave him the spark of life, making him fully human."

"But what of the serpent? I do not believe it was evil," she broke into his story again, impatient to hear it all.

"SSSSSSSSSSSSSSsssssssssssss!" he hissed, teasingly into her face. She recoiled, laughing merrily.

"The serpent was not evil at all! Sophia sent the serpent to be teacher to Adam and Eve. Through the serpent, they would be able to attain knowledge, achieving their full humanity—and putting them on a level close to the power of Jehovah. They would come to know they were not just his slaves, but of Divine origin themselves."

"Jehovah would not have liked that," the woman declared.

"Indeed. He was jealous that they had eaten of the fruit of the tree of Good and Evil. It meant they had the power of knowledge. He was filled with envy, and determined to punish Adam and Eve. He expelled them from the Garden of Eden, forced men to toil and women to labor in childbirth."

"So Yahweh is not the true Creator God?"

"No, the Creator God and Sophia, who together created Yahweh, are the true father and mother of humanity. But you must remember the Monad—being the True God—and the Aeons are above them all."

"Yes," she sighed, "this is nearly identical to what I believe, and what Yeshua secretly told me. But it is not what Paul would claim is true. His God is Yahweh, the One God, who has no female counterpart. Paul tells people Yeshua is Divine, one with the Father, Yahweh. I know full well, Yeshua is human! But many times he insisted we are all part of God.

109

"Do you not see how Paul's Roman religion sets us apart from our own divine origins?" Her face became angry now. "He has cut us off from God!"

James, the Joseph of Arimathea quickly moved to her side, bending down to hold her gently by the shoulders. "You must let go of that anger," he soothed her, "as my brother would want you to do. Remember, each person comes to awareness of his or her personal relationship with God by seeking it within himself; not by blindly accepting Paul's teachings. There is little you can do to stop Paul from preaching what he believes. But I can assure you, what your mission has accomplished is to plant the seed of truth in fertile soil. It will grow. Even if it is cut down by grim reapers, it will continue to grow throughout the generations.

"Be calm now, know I love and honor you. Let us rest." He smiled hopefully. "Perhaps Yeshua will visit us both tonight." So saying, he walked over to where the donkey was tethered and gave the animal a measure of grain. Then the Joseph spread his cloak upon the ground and prepared to lie down upon it.

"No, brother James," she protested, "lay some of these furs beneath your cloak that you might sleep more comfortably."

Gratefully, he took some furs to rearrange his bed.

By the time the moon had risen to shed her light into the cavern, they both lay peacefully dreaming.

* * * * *

It took us longer than anticipated to get on the road to Minerve the next morning. Ross, as usual, was up before the birds and off to the top of the hill to watch the sunrise, but the rest of us, tired from late night discussion, were moving slowly. Ross never seems to get tired.

Eventually, fortified with coffee and good French bread and cheese, we left for Minerve, the four of us packed tightly into the little green Renault.

It was market day in the nearby town of Olonzac, and although we arrived near mid-morning, there were still plenty of marvelous products from the countryside for sale. Most particularly, the olive vendor attracted our attention. On his table were more varieties of olives than we had ever seen—green, black, herbed, oil cured, brine cured, Niçoise, Greek, stuffed, unstuffed—featuring the queen of them all, a small green ripe olive flavored with *herbes de Languedoc*, a specialty of the region, superb!

By the time we departed Olonzac for Minerve, our shopping bags were not only full of olives; but also bread, nuts and cheeses, and of course, local wine. And Ross had found a memory of his childhood, licorice sticks, at the bakery. By licorice sticks I don't mean those long chewy ropes of black and of red, (why do they call that red stuff 'licorice' anyway? It doesn't taste like licorice at all!) No, these were real *sticks*. Roots, I suppose, or twigs of a licorice bush. You chew the end until it resembles a worn out paintbrush, then cut it off and start again. It has a very pleasant flavor, but looks funny. In the picture Karol took of us chewing on them, we appear to be smoking strange, possibly illegal, skinny brown cigarettes.

Heading north the short drive to Minerve, Peter only had enough time to fill us in on the background of Cathar persecution. The belief system of the Cathars, he said, could wait until lunchtime.

"Now, understand," he began, from the back seat where, map in hand, he fulfilled the duties of both tour guide and navigator, "by the time of the Albigensian Crusades, the Cathars had become a strong religious force in Languedoc. The Albigensian Crusade actually took its name from the city of Albi, north of Carcassonne, although it began with the sack of Béziers in 1209 CE."

"Why did the Roman church suddenly decide to wipe out the Cathars? Or was it so sudden, really?" Ross was trying to get a feeling for the flow of history.

"No, it wasn't sudden," answered Peter. "Pope Innocent III tried to convince them to convert first, but those stubborn Cathars refused to change their tune. All attempts at reconciliation with Pauline organization and dogma were unsuccessful.

"This 'heretic' group had been a thorn in the side of Orthodoxy for more than a hundred years before they were declared *anathema* by the Church in 1179. But it wasn't until thirty years later, after all attempts at negotiation failed, that the Roman church finally took action."

Peter was consulting the map while he talked. "Turn left at the next intersection."

"OK," Karol nodded. "But what was it that finally precipitated their action?" She wheeled the Renault onto a country road, following the course of a river between steep sided hills.

"It was a single incident. When the Count of Toulouse, Raymond VI, failed to prosecute the heretics under his rule in 1207, Pope Innocent III excommunicated him. Unfortunately for the Cathars, one of Raymond's knights killed the papal legate who delivered the excommunication orders. This upset the already frustrated Pope, to the point that he proclaimed a crusade against them in 1209. It lasted until 1244."

"Thirty-five years?" Ross questioned, thinking how quickly we can wage a war in the world today. Drop a bomb—over and out!

"Were the Cathars all exterminated by 1244, then?"

"Most of them. But the stream of Catharism continued to wind its way unnoticed, underground, through the centuries. Even up to the present day. The modern Cathar church in North America is called 'The Assembly of Good Christians.'"

"Amazing. I had no idea there was a modern Cathar church."

"Nor I."

"Nor I."

"Does this car have an echo?"

112

"Be serious, Peter. We're trying to learn something here. They really were good Christians, weren't they?"

"Yes, Karol. They were known for an exemplary lifestyle. Even those who persecuted the Cathars could find no fault with the way they lived their Truth."

"But what actually happened in Béziers?" I interjected, wanting to know the whole story. "We understood the entire city was put to the torch and everyone killed. We could still feel bad vibes when we drove through there."

Peter looked up from the map.

"We're almost at Minerve. Turn right up the hill....Béziers, you said? Well, at the time of the crusade against it, about 200 Cathars were living in the City. The crusaders gave the Catholic townspeople the opportunity to get out and leave the Cathars to their fate, but the townspeople refused to leave or give up the Cathars. They took an oath to defend them.

"So on July 22, 1209, Béziers was taken, on Saint Mary Magdalene's Feast Day. Since the Cathars had a tradition of Mary Magdalene as the concubine of Jesus, and that tradition was apparently honored throughout Béziers, the Orthodox church felt the town's destruction was fit reprisal for the people having 'insulted her' through this heretical belief."

"And they killed everybody"

"Men, women and children. Even the priests. When asked how the crusaders would know the Catholic townspeople from the heretics, the Pope is said to have told them 'Kill them all. God will know his own.' And then they burned down the town."

"How many people?" Ross inquired.

"Between 15,000 and 20,000."

"And what nasty knight was in command of the crusaders?"

"His name was Simon de Montfort, a ruthless, unconscionable predator."

"Ah," I sighed. "Man's inhumanity to man. How could they have called that Pope *Innocent?*"

113

"An oxymoron of sorts," Karol observed. "Peter, this looks like the turnoff to Minerve."

"Right. Pull into that parking lot by the bridge."

As we got out of the car, an unmistakable fragrance enveloped us.

"Wine!" Ross exclaimed. "The whole blinking town smells like wine!"

We sniffed.

It did.

The harvest was in, the first pressing of the grapes had finished, and now wagons full of fermenting, squashed red grapeskins were depositing their loads in the great Minervois presses to be transformed into *grappa*. Nothing is wasted. Not even the smell. It becomes the rich, heady, autumn perfume of Languedoc.

Walking to the edge of the parking lot, we found ourselves looking over a deep gorge, at red tiled roofs on the other side. A stone church, crowning the town at about our eye level, surmounted houses spilling down the sides of cliffs, ending where the drop-off became too sheer to support buildings. As a town, isolated on a rocky island, surrounded by the moat of the river's deep gorge, Minerve looked impregnable.

However, a large information sign by the parking lot informed us that Minerve had been captured by Simon de Montfort's troops in 1210. He used catapults to batter the town and destroy the town's well, its principal water supply. After the well was destroyed, Minerve capitulated. The village people were spared, but 140 Cathars who had taken refuge in the town were burnt at the stake.

"Where does that river go?" Ross asked, peering down. It seemed to disappear into the face of a cliff.

"Once we cross that bridge, we'll know," called Karol, halfway there already. And what a bridge! It had the appearance of a Roman aqueduct, great stone arches plunging support columns into the riverbed a hundred feet below. Looking over the side

114

with Ross, we could see the river disappearing into a natural tunnel below us. A paved pathway led from the town down into the gorge, winding along the river's edge as far as we could see.

"I'm going down there." Ross was getting excited. "I want to collect some of that water." He picked up the pace, moving towards the far end of the bridge, backpack bobbing.

"He collects water from sacred places and mixes them all together," explained Peter. "and then he uses them in ceremony." We trotted after Ross, catching up just as he reached the bridge's other end.

Although the rest of us were eager to browse around the city, we followed Ross into the gorge right away. Below the town were fields and fruit trees bordering an ancient cemetery. There we sat on a stone wall and rested, while Ross collected his holy water. This accomplished, we walked together along the river, until a great stone visage, emerging from a cliffside boulder, stopped us in our tracks.

Huge, sightless, chalky white eyes above a bearded face carved into a boulder stared out across the chasm. They gazed in silent, eternal, ghostly rebuke at the shadow of that evil crusader, Simon de Montfort, who had brought tragedy to Minerve.

Time out for lunch, we decided, sobered by the sight.

A couple of colorful umbrellas protruding over the cliff's top level seemed to beckon us onward and upward. After puffing up the pathway we did in fact find a restaurant perched precariously over the gorge.

On its terrace, white marble-topped tables welcomed us. Very soon ours was bearing an artist's still life: a brown salt glazed pottery wine pitcher, a carafe of crystal cool water fired by a brilliant shaft of light, and four glasses half filled with ruby red wine, glowing like jewels on their white marble canvas.

While our lunch was being prepared in a cave-like kitchen off the terrace, we basked in that warm autumn sunlight. There seemed no lingering trace of Cathar persecution here. All was peaceful, the sky a cobalt blue, the air heavy with grape perfume.

115

"I expected a place reeking of misery," I observed, turning my face towards the warm sun and unbuttoning my jacket.

"The energies have been balanced," Ross stated.

"Just how do you mean that, Ross?" Karol questioned.

"I mean enough people have come to this place to promote its healing, that residual negativity has been cancelled out."

"Sort of like mixing complementary colors creates gray?" I suggested. "Each color neutralizes the other. Good energy neutralizes bad?"

"Right mate. That's why I gather the waters of sacred places. They carry good energy to places that need it."

I broke off a piece of fresh *baguette* that had been placed by our tabletop still life. "That's what you have been doing, isn't it, Peter?" I asked, inhaling its fragrance before popping it into my mouth. "I mean, you've been traveling all over the world with your beautiful Aquarian Cross, bringing and balancing energy wherever you go.

"Remember when you placed it on top of the long barrow at Wayland's Smithy in England last summer? I took a picture of the sun striking the gold of its *vesica piscis,* the two interlocking circles in the center of its equal arms. Incredibly moving."

Peter smiled. "Yes, that was a beautiful moment. It was that same cross I carried from Jerusalem to Glastonbury. I planted it by the thorn tree of Joseph of Arimathea, as a symbol of the Christ Energy moving from East to West. And yes, I have carried it around the world."

"Beautiful symbolism," Karol remarked.

Soon we found ourselves moving into deep mealtime conversation; and once more, Peter became the teacher.

"Time to tell us what the Cathars believed, " I reminded him between bites of baguette.

"Yes, of course." He paused, collecting his thoughts, while our sandwiches were placed in front of us.

"Well first of all, they were Gnostics. That is, they followed the Gnostic tradition of believing that people could achieve integration with the Creator through personal enlightenment, not by blindly following blindly dogmatic rituals of the Orthodox church. And, as I have said, by rejecting the hierarchy of the Roman church, they felt justified in refusing to obey that authority."

"A fatal mistake." I added.

"Not in their minds, really. They were willing to die for their beliefs, because they felt the human body was an evil prison. To die meant to be released from it. That is why they went so willingly into the flames."

"Yes, but not all of them were that holy, were they?" I find it hard to hate the body so much as to willingly sacrifice it. Especially so painfully.

"No. There were two classes of Cathars. The great majority of them were lay people, 'believers,' who led reasonably ordinary lives as weavers and craftspeople. It was the 'pure ones,' the *Parfaits*, who were the holy people. These initiates led very ascetic lives, supported by the laity who supplied them with daily necessities.

"The Parfaits were vegetarians. They lived a celibate life, dressed simply in dark blue gowns, and were master adepts, able to utilize unseen energies to perform their special ceremonies. And they believed women were equal with men, except that women were not allowed to preach."

"So what were their special ceremonies?" Karol was passing the basket of omnipresent and delicious *frites*. "They were Christians, but did they believe in marriage, baptism and communion like the Roman church?"

"No," answered Peter, putting some fries on his plate. They only had one sacrament. It was called *The Consolamentum.* We were just talking about energy. This ritual was a kind of laying on of hands that transmitted tremendous energy to the recipient. It seems to have been as powerful as the descent of the Holy Spirit on the Apostles at Pentecost."

"Who received that sacrament, and who performed it?" The basket had arrived at Ross, who dipped into it, making a generous pile next to his sandwich. "Could anyone receive it?"

"No, not at all. It was reserved for two special occasions. One was when a person was about to die, to assist him or her to reunion with the Divine."

"Sort of like Last rites?"

"Sort of, but from what people who witnessed it said, it seems to have been a far more powerful transmission of energy."

"And the other occasion?"

"This was when a believer was initiated as a Parfait. And it was only Parfaits who could administer the Consolamentum."

Peter touched his napkin to his mouth, pushing his empty plate aside, leaning forward intently as if to imprint the information indelibly onto our minds.

"The Cathars were dualists. They believed that everything about the material world was evil and that only the spiritual world was good. Everything was seen as a battle between those two polarities. Mankind's task was, through a life of purity, to free the spirit from the body so that it could eventually return to the Light. Lay people realized they would have to return to life many times in order to achieve the level of the Parfaits, a level that would lead the Parfaits directly to the Light upon death."

"You can see why they were not afraid of death," remarked Karol, taking the last sip from her ruby cup.

"Not only not afraid, they welcomed it. And because they were adepts, it is likely the Parfaits were able to make that transformation painlessly. One of their beliefs was that Jesus was too Divine to be a material person. Therefore, he could not really have been crucified and resurrected."

Ross laughed. "That must have riled the Roman church a little bit."

"Exactly. But the Cathars could have gotten away with their 'heretical' beliefs if they had not opposed the power of Rome. It was really politics that did them in."

"Religion *is* politics," I repeated my earlier observation.

"Quite so. But the Cathars' belief system, being dualistic, contributed to their passing. In the evolution of spirituality, they had not yet reached the point that they understood all is One. Good and Evil are two faces of the same coin, and the journey is to integrate both the dark and the light into oneness. Completeness. The All."

It seemed a good place to end our discussion. After paying for lunch, we walked to the top of the town, passing the grape presses, visiting a sculptor's studio (it was he who sculpted the great stone face by the river) and some small curio shops. We visited briefly with a group of artists painting the town, so to speak. (Bad pun. I do that a lot.)

All the while, the sun shone brightly.

But when we arrived at the church, darkness seemed to cloud the happiness in our hearts. We had read about the martyrs' monument, wanted to see it. But a roof was being repaired in the church school next to the monument, and nobody was allowed to walk up to it because big chunks of tile were falling into the courtyard.

Talk about Armageddon! It was as if the sky were falling around us. Clouds of dust rose from the earth. Loud noise blasted our ears as each chunk hit the pavement. Watching from a distance we experienced the brutal pain that had taken place on that very spot. Shouts of battle, burning pyres, searing flesh, screams of anguish, seemed very real in that moment of time.

It was well we were not allowed upon the very spot of martyrdom. It would have been unbearable.

The Martyrs' monument, a large stone visible from the street, was pierced by the image of a dove. Through that dove-shaped window, we could glimpse the sky.

The dove.

Symbol of the soul.

A portal through which the souls of Cathar martyrs escaped into the blue, blue sky beyond earth's bounds.

Joyously flying to reunion with the Light.

SIRAN:
Karol at the Dolmen des Fados

Chapter Thirteen

The Dolmen

* * * * *

As the two old friends lay sleeping, a swirling wind howled into the cave, blowing dust and dead leaves into little dancing spirals around them. The donkey brayed in terror, arousing the slumbering pair.

"Steady, boy," the man tried to calm the beast, rising to comfort him. "There is nothing to fear."

But even as he uttered these words, a dark shape emerged from within the whirlwind, a cold, dreadful mist— roiling and writhing along the floor, expanding to the walls, threatening to envelop everyone within the cavern in suffocating terror.

"Yeshua!" screamed the woman. "Save us from this horrible thing!"

A great burst of light shriveled the darkness into a melting pool of black; and suddenly it was no more.

From the light stepped forth a familiar form—the Master, arm raised, holding a chalice from which streamed forth living, liquid light. It undulated around his figure, bubbling through it, fragmenting into an aura of dancing sparkles.

"I am never far from you. Fear not."

"Yeshua! Brother!" The Joseph knelt in awe. "It is truly you!" He reached to touch the resplendent figure.

"Nay, James, touch me not. This body is but a manifestation of soul—an illusion, formed only by energy of the Cosmos. It will be the same for you some day.

"Yet, you can see me, converse with me, and I can work what you call magic, for I have not relinquished my power. I can take you to mysterious places to see amazing things, so that you may understand the thread of life, which connects us all."

"Take us, then, brother, wherever you will."

At the request of his brother, the dazzling figure tipped the chalice in his hand, spilling its light over the two figures on the floor. Immediately they too became forms of light, leaving their mortal bodies where they lay—she sitting upright on her bed, he, kneeling on the floor.

Instantly their spirit bodies were transported to a desert place. Three huge pyramids lined the horizon, against a night sky littered with stars. The pyramids reflected the position of three great stars in the Heavenly Hunter's belt— As above, so below.

"I remember this place," claimed the Joseph as they found themselves before a rock-hewn temple piercing the face of a huge cliff. "It is near here I was born, while we were living in Egypt. It is here I used to play with you, elder brother, throwing pebbles into the center of a circle drawn in the sand. Do you remember?"

"Yea, brother, it is so."

As for the woman, although she had never been in this place before, it felt so very familiar…. She wondered why this could be.

"Let us enter the temple," Yeshua urged. Instantaneously they were inside a great hall penetrating the cliff, the darkness within becoming illuminated by their own light-filled spirits. Columns on each side supported the ceiling, forming a corridor through which they moved to enter a small opening in the end wall, leading in turn into a special room.

122

At the end of that room was a stone bench, upon which were seated two bronze figures sheathed in gold.

"Isis and Osiris!" She bowed before them—her body of light responding in a very normal fluid motion, rather to her surprise.

"Yes," affirmed Yeshua. "Come, my love. Here we shall await the dawn."

Magically transfixing Joseph of Arimathea in his position— kneeling before the bench in adoration— the Master and his wife found themselves inside the gilded statues, looking out through shining, jet black eyes.

Moments, perhaps hours, passed as the three spirits rested in trance. Slowly, stars faded in the night, and the Sun God Ra began to rise over the horizon. Outside the temple, they could hear chanting of priests and priestesses, the sound rising in volume as Ra moved higher into the sky. With a final burst, the disc of fire pulled free from earth, and the chanting erupted into loud cheering. "Welcome back, Blessed Holy Ra, True God of the Heavens and the Earth!"

At the end of the temple, one huge beam of sunlight, streaking through the colonnade, pierced the small room, and burst upon the faces of the two statues enthroned in its farthest wall. Suddenly, the statues became pure golden light, reflections of the Sun God Ra himself.

Spring had begun. The cycle of Life had continued without interruption. Life-giving waters would once again flood the land, impregnating the soil in sacred marriage.

The people would prosper.

All would be well.

As above, so below.

* * * * *

123

The feeling of Apocalypse, the sky falling at the monument to the Martyrs, left us with little desire to further explore Minerve. We had visited most of it anyway, since in October, many of the shops and restaurants are closed for the season. And we had experienced what we had come for, a firsthand encounter with that part of history. It chilled our flesh.

Drawing light jackets around us, we trotted back across the aqueduct-like bridge, to pile back into the Renault and take off for Siran.

"It's still early," said Ross, who never seemed to wind down. "Why don't we go visit the dolmen we've been passing on the road east of Siran?"

"The Dolmen des Fados?"

"Yeah. That's it." His "Yeah" sounded like yay-ah.

This time it was my turn to drive. "Sure," I agreed. Navigator, get us there. Philippe says people dance naked in the Dolmen at the full moon."

Karol laughed. "Thank goodness it's not a full moon tonight!"

"And what would you do if it were?" Ross nudged her shoulder from his position in the back seat.

"You'll never know, seeing as it's not a full moon."

"Come, now, children," Peter chided good naturedly, "Quit the play."

Less than an hour later, he obligingly steered us to a little pull-off (he calls it a way-by) beside a road sign pointing to the Dolmen Des Fados. It was invisible from the highway. All we could see was a tree-covered hill rising out of flat vineyards.

"It must be up there," Ross indicated the hill with a nod of his head.

So off we trudged, sampling leftover grapes, through the vineyard toward the mysterious hill.

You never see a field of wheat, or oats around the Languedoc. It's always grapes. The area has but one major agriculture: grapes— and but one product: wine. It's scary to

124

think of what might happen if the crop were to be wiped out by a natural disaster. There was a preview in 1999, when floods washed entire vineyards down from the hills into the valleys below. Best not to think about it too much.

"Must be the right place," I shouted to the others lagging behind, "here's a sign." I read it out loud, translating into English for the benefit of Karol and Ross.

"Historic Monuments," said the headline. Beneath, in large letters: *"Dolmen Des Fados."* The following lines read: *"Megalithic Tomb built more than 5000 years ago. Thank you for respecting the Monument and the area around it."*

It was signed *"The Mairie of Pépieux."*

"PÉPIEUX!" sang Karol.

"PÉPIEUX!" I echoed. We loved that name. Every time we passed by signs to the village of Pépieux we sang it out. "Pay-pee YUH" is as close as I can get phonetically in English.

"It does have a rather musical ring," Peter muttered wryly, rolling his eyes over at a puzzled Ross.

"No matter," I rejoined, "you guys wouldn't understand. Let's climb on up."

Waiting at the top of the hill was a sight to take breath away and leave silly banter behind. A dolmen is a huge, flat stone balanced on top of a couple of other megaliths.

This was not just a dolmen.

"It's a long barrow!" I shouted. Look!

At our feet lay a long chamber, dug into the earth. It was possibly about 30 to 40 feet long, 7 or 8 feet wide and about as deep. Part of it was roofed by a great stone slab, perched on four support megaliths built into the walls. Along the sides, other megaliths were interspersed between neatly laid horizontal stones, suggesting more of the barrow had been roofed over in much earlier times.

Was it an ancient tomb? Yes, but we guessed it had an additional function, when we saw two waist-high partitions bisecting the long chamber. The southern one had obviously been shaped into a circular opening, although much of it had broken away. About 10 feet to the north of it, two stones formed another partition, with a narrow space between them. Again, 10 feet to the north a bench was built into the northern wall of the chamber. I sat down on it and looked straight through the two partitions. It was like looking down the sights of a rifle.

Imagine sitting on that bench, with the chamber entirely roofed over. Perhaps it was dawn of the Winter Solstice, when the rising sun was entering the tomb. As you watch from your seat on the bench, the rising sun's rays spill past the two partitions, casting a shaft of golden light directly upon your face. Perhaps you are a holy man, wearing a golden mask. Imagine the other holy men kneeling in adoration. *Imagine....Yes, imagine....*

Peter breaks into my daydream. "We must do ceremony here," he states, "when you are through with your journey."

Leaving my realm of creative thought, I observed Karol and Ross above me. They were standing on opposites sides of the roof rock, both hands touching it, heads bowed in meditation. Peter was holding the Aquarian cross he wears around his neck to the late afternoon sunlight, which glinted off its gold surface.

It seemed we were all mentally preparing for a ritual.

"Yes, of course," I responded. "Peter, please lead us."

After Ross poured a little of his sacred water onto the floor of the chamber, the four of us joined hands in a circle around it. Male, female, male, female. "Balances the energy," Peter explained.

"Let us start by toning." His clear voice mellowed into a round sound.

"Ommmmmmmmmmmmmmmmmmmmmmmmmmmmmmm."

"Ommmmmmmmmmmmmmmmmmmmmmmmmmmmmmmm," we joined him, each person's individual voice quality blending into a rich tapestry of vibration. Toning with our eyes closed, our ears perceived the sound growing, echoing off the walls of the ancient barrow, spiraling into the sky.

Silence.

Slowly we began circling to the left, clockwise, still holding hands. Then faster, whirling the energy into the center.

Slowing.

Stopping.

Circling to the right, now, anti-clockwise, eyes still closed, whirling the energy in the opposite direction into the center.

Slowing.

Stopping.

A few moments of silent prayer, then Peter opened his eyes and said, "Now I will teach you the Cathar Mantra.

Repeat after me."

"I AM THE FOUNTAIN OF LIGHT."

"I am the fountain of Light."

"I AM THE TRUTH."

"I am the Truth."

"I AM THE UNIVERSE."

"I am the Universe."

"I AM ALL CONSCIOUSNESS."

"I am All Consciousness."

"I AM ALL-BEING."

"I am All-Being."

"I AM THE SPIRIT OF LOVE-
DEEP, UNCONDITIONAL AND FOREVER."

"I am the spirit of Love—Deep, Unconditional and Forever."

"MY GIFT TO THE LIGHT WHICH IS AROUND ME,"

"My gift to the Light which is around me,"

"IS THE SPARK OF LIFE."

"Is the Spark of Life."

"I CARRY IT FREELY, GENEROUSLY, AND IN PURITY OF SOUL."

"I carry it Freely, Generously, and in Purity of Soul."

"AND THUS IT SHALL BE,"

"And thus it shall be,"

"FOREVER AND EVER."

"Forever and Ever."

We stood silently for a long moment, while the sound of our voices faded into the woods around us, carrying on into infinity. Face elevated toward the sky, Peter then recited the Lord's Prayer—not in familiar English, but in the Aramaic language Jesus himself spoke.

Another moment of silence, while the sacred syllables floated out over the earth.

Eyes smiling, Peter turned to face Karol. "Now we shall perform the Cathar greeting, a kiss on both cheeks, followed by deep eye contact."

He grasped her lightly by the shoulders. She reached to hold him in the same way. They kissed each other's cheeks, then gazed deeply into each other's eyes. Ross and I did the same. Afterwards, we greeted each of the others in turn.

Gazing into each others' eyes, filling them and drinking deeply of pure spiritual love, became a moment so profound, that it showed us, for a few minutes, a tiny glimpse of what the Cathars must have felt for each other. With such love in their hearts, it must have been easier to surrender their bodies to the flames.

Each of us made a private prayer of thanks for this moment before we walked slowly down the hill, elevated in spirit, glad to end the day on such a beautiful note.

Whether or not the good energy carried over onto our dinner plates, I don't know; but our meal was so colorful and delicious I climbed a stair to take a picture of the table from above.

Black glass plates on a gaily-colored tablecloth bore white rice and an array of sautéed fresh, mixed vegetables. Keeping the plates company on the tabletop were three kinds of olives, two kinds of wine, a sliced white fennel salad with sweet red pepper strips on top, and dark brown bread—*pain de campagne,* "country bread".

It had been a day filled with a full range of emotions. Surely the spirits of the Magdalene and the Cathars were hovering near, drawing ever closer.

I dreamed restless dreams that night, a kaleidoscope of sights, sounds, feelings. Wandering through the chaos of those dreams, the four of us walked steadily forward, apparently making some sort of pilgrimage.

We were clad in long, dark blue robes.

MONTSÉGUR:
Ruined Ramparts

Chapter Fourteen

MONTSÉGUR, LAST CATHAR STRONGHOLD

* * * * *

The golden sun God of Provence streamed deep into the cave, bathing their faces in light. Not the golden arrow of Ra— but to the couple awakening, it seemed an extension of a dream not yet left behind.

"Life has returned for another day, dear brother," the woman whispered. "Let us arise to greet the dawn."

They shook off the wonder of the night, splashing water from the cistern upon their faces, drinking in its cool refreshment. The man refilled the donkey's bowl, giving the beast a handful of grain.

"Be patient, old friend," he patted its forehead and scratched behind one ear. "We shall soon have you back in your stall for a well earned rest."

Together, they walked to the meditation rock to silently pray. After a few moments, he lifted his head and hands to the sun, intoning "… and thus it shall be, forever and ever."

"So be it," she affirmed.

The Joseph settled on the ground beside her, breaking a piece of leftover bread, handing her a morsel.

"Dear sister," he began, looking up into her eyes, "take and eat this, for it shall be our last meal together."

Startled, she could not respond, but took the bit of bread, holding it in her hands, sensing great importance in this moment.

"My true purpose in coming to see you was to share a few last moments, to see you laugh with joy in this life, for death is drawing us both close to her breast. But we shall soon be together again, joined in God's celestial presence."

She bowed her head, still silent, knowing what he said was true. Her heart confirmed it.

"Last night, when Yeshua came, I felt the veil begin to thin," he continued. "I felt him drawing me near. I became part of the All, in another form, and you did too."

She nodded, understanding his words, breaking her silence at last. "I have felt the mysteries of these past few days were preparing me, but I did not consider that you, dear James, were close to that threshold as well."

"I believe the end is near for me, because a man who hates me has become the high priest in Jerusalem. Ananus-Demas not only hates, but also fears me. If I return to Jerusalem, he will probably cause me to be stoned to death."

"Why so, James? You have done no harm. And you have been faithful to the Way."

"Exactly so, dear friend. He thinks the Way subversive to all Jews, and I know he fears the growing power of Yeshua's followers."

"The answer is simple. Stay here in Gaul. Do not return to Jerusalem!" Passion inflamed her words, coloring her cheeks.

"Do you think Yeshua would have heeded that same advice, knowing he was to be denounced and crucified?"

She hung her head, ashamed. "I did indeed thus counsel him to stay in Bethany, out of love for him, my husband and my consort."

"And out of love for you and all mankind, he suffered much, although he did not die as people wish to believe."

She sat quietly, the crust of bread in one hand, remembering his pain, and hers.

"*I must return to Jerusalem,*" *he said softly, touching her sleeve to bring her attention back to the moment.* "*I must return, for the faithful face persecution, and I am their leader. They were his sheep—but I have become their shepherd. Now that Yeshua is gone, they are confused and know not what to believe. For years after he departed the sheep walked straight ahead, through a green valley. But powers have been raised up against them. I have been too often away. They need me.*"

"*I understand. You were the Joseph; now you are the David. It is your duty.*"

"*And last night confirmed my suspicions. Death will overtake me soon.*"

"*Oh, James—what is this thing death? I fear it and yet I welcome it!*"

"*It is but a curtain through which we pass, into another life, a life in which we move towards being united with the All, which is the Light. Death is but a rite of passage, no more real than the 'death' of Simon, when he became the Lazarus.*"

"*You mean his excommunication? His ritual death?*"

"*Of course, and once he came back to life, nothing was ever the same for him again. Is this any different than leaving this body and moving into new life?*"

"*I suppose not,*" *she agreed.* "*I remember when Agrippa excommunicated our brother Simon. He had been such a hotheaded zealot, dealing death and destruction to the conquering Romans! So they put him in the Abraham cave at Qumran for four days, dressed in grave clothes, a ritual death.*"

"*Yes, and do you remember what happened?*"

"*Of course. Mary Helena and I were there with Yeshua, who was acting as a priest, when he released Simon from the tomb under the order of Agrippa's rival, Antipas. You should have seen him! So bewildered when he emerged, blinking at the bright light, unwashed, dusty, smelling like a pig!"*

"And yet Helena received him into her arms?"

"Of course. He was her love, her partner in the sacred marriage, just as Yeshua is mine. But he was really confused as to why Yeshua should defy the authorities, taking the role of a priest to command the stone be rolled away."

"It was a big risk."

"I know. Perhaps if he had not raised Simon into "Lazarus" they would not have condemned him to suffer on the cross."

"Perhaps, but he knew he was supposed to suffer."

"Yes, and to die. But he did not!"

"And yet, dear sister, his life was changed forever, much as was Simon's. Is this not death?"

"It is so," she acknowledged. "Simon became the Lazarus, our brother and friend, who accompanied us to these shores in Gaul. Yeshua became a legend. People could not believe his appearances were real— in body, not in spirit. They made him into a God."

"Death brings rebirth," James stated. "All kinds of death create new life, even symbolic death."

The old man rose painfully to his knees. Replacing her two hands together around the bit of bread, he pushed them towards her mouth. "Take, then, and eat, and I shall eat with you, as Yeshua taught us. Share this bread with me, for soon we, too shall begin new lives."

* * * * *

I arose early the next day, just as dawn was breaking. Still full of the night's restless dreams, and brimming with new information, I wanted time by myself to let it overflow into the pages of my journal. My precious journal, safe deposit box for daily impressions, seems to be the only way I can clear out enough mind space to absorb all the new data coming in. So I put on the coffeepot and settled down at the kitchen table.

"Rennes-le-Château, " I wrote, "is not really about treasure, unless you see Mary Magdalene as treasure indeed. We saw her there in the center of her power, hidden, secret. We see her everywhere, in the softness of the vineyards and warmth of the sun. But we also have seen mankind's cruel efforts to suppress her energy.

"It's her turn to come to the fore again. Perhaps we are in the flow of that energy, transmuting pain to pleasure...."

I put down my pen, rising to fill my cup at the kitchen counter. *Everything is a secret,* I thought. *Everything is underground, from the meaning of the Black Madonna, to the coding of the parchments Saunière discovered and the secret knowledge of the Cathars. Even the Bible is said to be coded, and the documents discovered at Qumran, the Dead Sea Scrolls. Why? Is the truth too dangerous to bring out in the open?*

Back at the table, I kept writing. "...But perhaps we, and others, are doing what needs to be done. It has been prophesied that now is the time for secrets to be revealed, for old institutions to crumble, making way for the new...."

"G'day, mate." (G'dye, mite.) It was Ross, ready to welcome sunrise at the top of the hill, bouncing through the kitchen and out the door.

Unlikely revolutionaries, we, I thought, *two senior citizens, a bouncing Aussie and a tour guide. Well, I guess Peter fills the bill, but the rest of us...?*

Some inner voice broke in. *"We are all points of light,"* it softly whispered.

"Enough points of Light and you have fireworks."

By 9 o'clock the four of us, breakfasted and fully awake, set out again. This time, the plan for the day included climbing

135

Montségur, and then descending into the bowels of the earth to see prehistoric cave drawings. An "up and down day," one might wryly say.

First stop was at Olonzac again, to buy bread to accompany the olives and cheese from the refrigerator. You have to buy bread in a bakery in France. Although there are supermarkets, the only kind of bread we have found in them is a soft, sweet, white sort of biscuit.

You want crusty baguettes? You go to a bakery. You ignore the tempting sweets and chocolaty delicacies that call out to you, stoically refraining from saying "…and I'll have one of those too, *merci*." And walk out with your bread, feeling virtuous—and hungry for more.

Our hosts Philippe and Margaret had warned us the climb up Montségur would not be easy, so we wanted to be well supplied with food energy. Also, since we had to be at the Grotte de Niaux for the 2:30 PM tour, a leisurely lunch like the day before in Minerve, was out of the question.

Alors, packing the picnic goodies into the Renault's "boot,"—trunk to Yanks—we set off on another day's adventures.

Along the way, I read aloud what the guidebook had to say about Montségur, and Peter filled in the rest.

From the beginning of the Albigensian crusade against the Cathars, in 1209, thirty-four years elapsed before the siege of Montségur began. During those thirty-four years, many Cathars had fled to the fortress to escape persecution, concentrating about 500 souls on its rocky height.

It had become the headquarters of the Cathar religion and, most importantly, the refuge of their leaders. What was left of the Cathar remnant had dispersed into the caves and foothills of the Pyrenees, effectively ending their threat to French and Roman Catholic authorities, whose strong arm was the infamous Inquisition.

As with the sack of Béziers, the siege began with a single incident. A man named Pierre-Roger de Mirepoix, head of the garrison surrounding and protecting Montségur, was informed that two famous and much feared Inquisitors were on their way to Montségur with a group of nine men. Mirepoix sent a military party, who ambushed and killed the entire group. Naturally this pleased the independent, anti-French Monarchy people of Languedoc, but it unfortunately assured the end of the Cathar enclave at Montségur.

The French army established a siege at the foot of the mountain in May, 1243. It was not until nearly a year later that the citadel, which had been well supplied with food and water, fell. But before it did, a few "Pures" managed to descend the precipitous cliffs on ropes, bearing with them the famous Cathar treasure. When they were safely down, they built a small fire on a nearby hill to let the others know they had escaped. Only then did the Cathars surrender, to calmly meet their fate.

Those willing to confess and reject their "heretic" religion were spared. But on March 16, 1244, two hundred and ten condemned Cathars walked down the mountain singing, and into the huge bonfire on the field below.

"What was the treasure those men saved?" Ross asked Peter rhetorically, already anticipating the answer.

"Nobody knows. Of course it was probably not gold and jewels, or they would never have been able to get it down the cliffs. You will soon see why."

"Most probably parchments, sacred scripture, perhaps the inner secrets of the Religion," Ross surmised.

Peter was right. As soon as we came around the curve of a hill and spied Montségur in the distance, it was very apparent why nobody could carry a heavy chest down the slopes. The hill, known as a *pog*, rose vertically from the valley floor to a height of about 3700 feet above sea level, as high as the tallest peak in the Corbière Mountain Range to the east.

"Wow," said Karol. "Stop the car, Cinnie, I want to take a picture."

137

"That's not even the best view," chuckled Peter, who had been to Montségur before. "There's a better one from the parking lot." Not to be dissuaded, I pulled the car over onto a shoulder widened by other tourists, who had obviously wanted the same photo op. Three of us spilled out, aiming our cameras.

But Peter was right, of course. When we stopped our car in the parking area, the mountain loomed close before us, dominating the entire landscape.

"We're going to climb *that?*" muttered Karol, who had suffered a twisted ankle a few days earlier in Rennes-les-Bains. But she would not be left behind. She shouldered her backpack and set off across the flat field at the foot of the mountain.

"This is the burning field," Peter informed us, as we stopped for a moment to look. Someone previously had built a small fire on the grassy sward. Now it was a dead circle of ashes.

Nobody said anything.

It was too graphic a reminder.

About a hundred yards further on, at a fork in the rising path, a stele rose from its rock-built base. One side was embellished with a solar cross, an equal-armed cross set in a circle. The other side bore a design of three crosses above what looked to me like an abstract rendering of the Egyptian Eye of Horus. Beneath were inscribed in the language of Oc, the words: "To the Cathars, to the martyrs of pure Christian Love."

We paused a few moments in respect. Above the monument, the path steepened through overhanging brush. We labored upwards, not seeming to be gaining much ground on the mountain's flanks.

At the moment we began to feel really tired, a little shack appeared at the bottom of what turned out to be the *real* climb up. On the outside of the shack was a sign demanding twenty francs for the privilege of hauling ourselves up that knee-wrenching, thigh-burning path to the fortress on top. Inside the shack, a smiling old man held out his hand for the cash.

"They expect us to *pay* for this?" I groaned, shelling out the coins. The old man kept smiling. I suspect he enjoyed his job immensely, laughing at the lot of us.

But we were committed. Even Karol, who climbed a little more slowly, favoring her injured ankle, made it to the top, to be greeted by a group of cheering schoolchildren perched at the entrance to the ruin.

We did well. Less than an hour from the parking lot, we were finally within the massive fortress of Montségur.

Resting, looking around us, huge gray walls rose to form an empty enclosure, which reminded me of drawings I have seen of Noah's Ark. This impression was augmented later when, from my new vantagepoint perched on top of a rampart, I could observe the foundations and former connections to the wall of at least three levels within the fortress.

All gone now, of course. Peter said the whole place was ransacked after the surrender, by people searching for Cathar treasure. They tore down the inner buildings, stone by stone, finding nothing.

But what a view! Clutching an iron railing, I squirmed to the highest point of the rear wall, sitting, with trepidation, in a sort of depression where I could hold onto some rocks for emotional support. In front of me, the huge enclosure flowed into a second space— a rectangular, towered storeroom. Outside the walls, on all sides the mountain fell shear from within a few feet of its foundations. I could see at least a hundred miles in every direction.

Peter scrambled up beside me. "Breathtaking, isn't it?"

I nodded, fumbling with my camera case, afraid to let go with both hands at once.

"Did you know the fortress is oriented to the four cardinal directions? And it records the solstices, equinoxes and progression of the Zodiac?"

"No," I answered absently, intently focusing on the snow capped Pyrenees. "I didn't think the Cathars were particularly interested in that sort of thing."

"They weren't, but this was built on the foundations of a much older edifice, on a Pagan sacred site. Are you going to walk around on top of the walls?"

"Are you crazy?" I exploded, clutching the rock behind me for safety, as I rotated my camera to another direction.

"Just kidding." He pointed to an official sign nearby. "They wouldn't let you do it anyway."

Meanwhile, Karol was eating her sack lunch down in the enclosure, and Ross, who was obviously smitten with the place, was wandering around, taking photographs in every conceivable direction, of every conceivable thing.

Having recorded the magnificent 360 degree landscape on film, I sat quietly next to Peter for a while, just taking in the atmosphere of the place. Montségur is massive, huge, heavy. The energy seems very masculine, the pog almost phallic.

It was easy to imagine swords clanging against shields, boulders bombarding the ramparts, loud sounds of war and destruction. It seemed totally alien to what I had learned about the Cathars.

"These people were so peaceful. How could this have happened to them?"

Peter smiled ruefully. "Remember, it wasn't about their way of life. It was political. They got in the way of the French monarchy and the Roman church."

"Yes, I know. But it seems so unjust…."

"Justice wasn't part of it either."

"Nor compassion, I suppose. But they were human beings. How could they have calmly walked down this mountain and into the fires?"

"There is much that was mystical about these people," he confided. "The 'Pures' were Adepts."

"What do you mean, 'Adepts'?"

"They had deep, esoteric knowledge. They knew how to work with unseen energies, how to move in and out of

140

dimensional realities, and communicate with unseen forces. And of course they had no fear of death, for two reasons."

"Such as?"

"For one thing, they regarded the human body as sinful, base, vile and foul. Couldn't wait to get out of it, but only in a good way."

"What do you mean by good way?"

"One which would ensure they would not have to return again to this world for further purification. Martyrdom. They were believers in reincarnation."

"And the other reason?"

"Their belief in immortality of soul. Death was a transition, not an ending. Another step on their journey to the Light."

"But *pain!* Had they no fear of pain?"

"Adepts were practiced and disciplined in altered mental states. It would have been possible for them to place themselves in a trance-like state, impervious to pain. Many Adepts in today's cultures are capable of the same thing. You see them on television, in those 'Curious World' types of shows. Even in Western countries, shamanic trance is relatively common."

"Like the people who get together and walk across burning coals?"

"Yes. They are in altered states, in a sort of self-induced hypnosis. As for the Cathars, it could have been deep religious zeal, or simply a learned technique, probably shared by most esoteric initiates."

"Hmmm. This is hard for me to comprehend. I love life too much to want to leave it."

"Life is learning to let go."

"Very profound observation, Peter."

We sat a little longer, thinking, perhaps even remembering.

Abruptly, Peter came back to the present. He glanced at his watch. "We'd better pay attention to the time. Let's go back down and join the others."

"Right. Hold my hand, will you?"

141

We carefully scrooched from the top of the wall, to the descending stairs built into one side. Perhaps forty feet down the staircase, at the bottom, we threw our legs over an iron barrier (that kept nobody from climbing up,) to rejoin our companions.

Peter tapped his watch again.

"Just a little while longer, please?" Ross was in no hurry to leave. "Cynthia, would you please take a picture of me on the stairs over there?"

"Sure."

"Well OK, we can stay a bit longer if we eat our lunch in the car driving to the Grotte de Niaux."

Having already explored the inside of the ruin, I decided to take advantage of the extra time to walk around the outside. The path was necessarily narrow, since cliffs dropped off not more than ten feet from the bastion's foundations. Along the north side, the path sloped steeply towards oblivion, only a few feet from the wall. By then I was down on my hands and knees, grabbing onto bushes to keep from slipping.

I looked up at the fortress. Sunlight shining out from behind the ruin gave it a fiery glow. It was an opportunity that couldn't be lost. I grabbed the camera swinging near the ground from its strap around my neck. On all fours, I snapped the picture and, breathing a sigh of relief, hauled myself up to the wall and onto the wider path. When the photo was developed, a red glow envelops the bushes at the base of the ruin.

Fire remains in the heart of Montségur.

Later, after slipping, sliding and scrambling back down the mountain, skinning my knee on rocks made slick by billions of pilgrim feet, the four of us gathered around the ashes on the burning field to do a ceremony of remembrance honoring the martyrs.

Joining hands in a circle, moving clockwise, then counter clockwise, as we had done in the Dolmen, meditating, reciting the Cathar Mantra....

"I am the fountain of Light...
"I am the Truth...

142

…Suddenly I feel unseen hands turning my head to the left and upward.

... I am compelled to open my eyes.

…My gaze falls directly on the fortress atop the mountain.

…I know it is the last time I will see my refuge.

…I feel the heat of burning wood beneath my feet, but experience no pain.

...I smell smoke, burning flesh, but hear no cries.

...My soul flies up in shimmering waves, a dove taking flight to the Light.

...I am singing.

… *"I am the Spirit of Love—deep, unconditional and forever.*

… *"My gift to the Light which is around me*

… *"Is the spark of Life.*

… *"I carry it Freely, Generously, and in Purity of Soul.*

… *"And thus it shall be*

… *"Forever and ever."*

Stunned silence.

I open my eyes. My companions, still holding hands in our circle, are respectfully sending loving support to this tear-stained, obviously *undone* friend.

"What is it, Cinnie?" Karol whispers, "What happened?"

I blink, still unsure of which reality I am in. "I had a vision," I explain in a shaky voice, dropping Ross and Peter's hands to pull a Kleenex out of my pocket. Distractedly, I wipe my eyes and blow my nose— rather embarrassingly loudly.

It draws the attention of several passers-by, but serves to relieve the tension of the moment. Faintly smiling with the others, I recover enough to tell them the details of my experience.

"It seemed so real! I could swear it was happening!"

Peter nods wisely. "I have had such visions too, Cynthia. Don't let them scare you. There is nothing to be afraid of. Just meditate on it, so you will eventually be able to understand its meaning. This has happened to teach you something."

"Right," Ross adds. "A place like Montségur is where such things can occur. There has been so much violence; all sorts of energies are still hanging around. The veil between realities is thin here."

"Yes, it must be," Karol agrees softly. "I saw rising waves of energy too. Sort of shimmering rainbow colors. It was very moving."

"Let us give each other the Cathar greeting," suggests Peter, knowing it would bring closure to the experience.

It was incredible.

More human warmth and love was transferred than I could ever describe. I felt totally supported by my friends.

The ritual greeting gentled raw emotion left from that unnerving vision. Through the kiss on both cheeks, and eye contact, my companions helped transform the experience into just a vivid memory. But such a memory!

So now it was up to me, to process the experience, in the awareness it happened to teach me something important.

But what?

What could such a vision have to tell me?

Who would believe…

…the very next day I was to find out.

Chapter Fifteen

CAVES OF INITIATION

* * * * *

Thoughtfully, the woman placed the bread James had given into her mouth. It seemed to melt away without the need to chew, and tasted sweet as honey. When she looked up from her thoughts, her friend was already packing his belongings onto the back of the patient donkey.

"You must leave so soon?" She suddenly longed for his companionship to last forever. Perhaps she had indeed been too long a hermit.

"Yes, it is time. But I shall return with others, to see you before I go to Jerusalem."

"Others? Which others? Mary Salome and Mary Jacoba have already been buried under the church we founded."

"You shall see, when I return," teased the Joseph of Arimathea as he gave his donkey a pat on its haunch. He approached the woman, pulling her gently upright.

They gave each other the customary farewell kiss on both cheeks. Looking deeply into his eyes, she begged, "Hurry back soon, brother, for I fear I shall not be here many more days."

"Very soon," he vowed, dropping his arms from her shoulders and taking up the donkey's reins. She walked with the pair until the path turned upon itself, dropping steeply

downward. Once more he kissed her lightly, this time on the forehead.

"I promise," he confirmed.

She watched until the man and beast could no longer be seen among the trees. Sighing, she walked back to her meditation rock and sank down upon it, not caring that her hair fell down across her face while she studied the pebbles by her feet.

What a mockery, she thought, picking one up and letting it drop close to another. The stones are content where they rest. They do not long for company. Yet I, who spent all these years in contented solitude find, strangely enough, that in this moment I yearn for companionship.

"IT IS TIME TO RECONNECT." Startled, she looked up, brushing back her long tresses to cast her glance about the ledge. From where did that familiar voice emanate?

"I am here, by the big rock. Do you not see me?"

Gazing in the direction of his voice, she saw the figure of Yeshua emerging from the rock's shadow. He looked so real! She scrambled to her feet and rushed to embrace him.

"Touch me not." There was an authority in his voice that stopped her in her tracks, facing him. "The time has not yet come."

"My love!" she spoke boldly from the hurt in her heart, "So many times we have touched each other! First in the Temple when you came to me for initiation, so many times when we were the sacred bride and bridegroom, and so often as husband and wife—why may I not embrace you now?"

"You are still flesh, while I am Spirit. When you shed your earthly body, joining me in Paradise, I promise you ecstasy beyond knowing. But until then, you would only touch a mirage, no more real than a trick of heat in the desert."

"Yet I can hear and see you." Her voice trembled.

"Yes, through Sound and Light. And it is through Sound and Light that I come to prepare you."

146

"To prepare me?" Anger rose to the surface. *"To teach me mysteries I do not understand? Are you certain this is my desire?"* Involuntarily, the figure of Yeshua stepped back, confronted by her anger.

"Struggling to understand, gives birth to Wisdom," he explained, *"and Wisdom gives birth to Understanding. It is the snake swallowing his tail, a perfect circle."*

Conscious of her evident distress, he extended his arm. *"Hold out your hand."* Into her outstretched palm he dropped a ring that had magically appeared in his fist. But the ring was real enough, manifestation of his words, a golden snake eating its own tail.

"Wear this ring. It will remind you that the process of learning to Understand, is part of the Circle of Wisdom. It is also a token of my promise to once again be your holy bridegroom when at last we are together for eternity."

Chastened, she slipped the ring onto her finger. It gleamed there in the sunlight, seeming to melt away her anger in the heat of its golden brightness.

"I accept your promise," she murmured softly. Then, more forcefully, *"But to help me in the Understanding, can you tell me more clearly of my purpose?"*

"I have already told you," he answered patiently. *"Before you enter my reality, you must recognize your part in the threads of life. Everyone who comes into this material world plays a part in creating the web that connects us all. Everyone's life has meaning, for every soul's journey affects everything else. It changes the whole. If you were not created on this earth, the future would be different."*

"You mean because I was born, the future will be different than if I had not been born?"

"Exactly."

"I am aware of my past and the present, Yeshua. You have already shown me a glimpse of the future, but I did not understand it."

"Then I shall show you more. Come."

She took a step toward him, but in less than the space of a breath they were by a beautiful river, looking up at a cliff with a cave in it, a cave different from her own. Once again she saw she had no body, though Yeshua was still present in a different form: a soft, radiant circle of light, pulsating like a heartbeat.

A small group of people, dressed in dark blue robes, was climbing a path towards the cave's entrance. In the center of the assemblage walked a young woman, barely entered into womanhood, clad in long white vestments.

"Follow those people," he told her.

"But how? I have no body."

"Just think, and you will be wherever you wish." So saying, the light which she knew to be Yeshua faded and disappeared, leaving her alone and uncertain.

I must trust, she thought, and wished herself to the mouth of the cave, just at the moment the group of people passed under an archway built of stones without mortar. She followed them, as they entered the cave, singing.

Ahead, she saw an altar, fashioned from a stone that she knew to be granite, quite different from the cavern's mother rock. One of the walls held a square niche, with a curtain obscuring its contents; while into another wall was hewn a man-sized pentacle, as deep into the wall as two hands placed side by side.

The blue-clad people had formed a circle around the woman in white, apparently instructing her in a language the woman observing could not understand.

This must be an initiation, she surmised, watching the group alternately speaking and singing. Curious about the veiled niche, she willed herself in front of it but could not move the curtain aside.

"It is the Holy Grail," whispered a voice that only she could hear. It was a man's voice, but not the familiar sound

of Yeshua speaking.

"Who is here?" she whispered back, although even if she had shouted, the others would not have been able to hear. She knew this, from her previous trip to the future.

"Who is here?" she whispered again, louder this time. She could see nobody but the religious ones performing their ceremonies.

"It is I, John."

"John? The Baptist?"

"Yea, truly."

"You are dead, beheaded through treachery!"

"Yea, truly."

"By what miracle are you here, John? And can you not show yourself to me?"

"Do you not know by now that you, yourself, cannot be seen?"

"Ah, yes," she whispered. "This is all so strange to me. But I have seen the Master, Yeshua with my own eyes."

"It is because he has willed himself to manifest in his Light Body. I cannot be seen because I must stay hidden. Though Yeshua and I parted long ago, we kept many of the same beliefs. My followers also were forced into exile. His Way and my Way were both God's Way. And yet it is another Way that persecutes us all."

"But why are you here, John?"

"I am a hidden truth for these people. They believe in my Word. I cannot protect them, but I can guide them. I am always near to them."

"Who are these people?"

"They are known as Good Christians, Good Men and Women. They follow the Way you brought to Gaul, but the church Paul founded hates them, and wishes to kill them all."

"And the Good Christians also honor you?"

Yes, but not overtly. They honor me through my Word. See that book on the granite altar? It is my book, called the

Book of John."

"I did not know you wrote a book."

"Truly it is my work, although others will say it is written by another John. Yeshua knew the truth, and he passed my words— through his— to these believers."

"I know this is the future, but what year I do not know."

"More than a thousand years have passed since your body lived upon this earth. There are also many other things you do not know. One of them is that they revere you too, but secretly. They honor you as the symbol of the Feminine. It is I who represents the Masculine."

"I? You say they honor me? But this is wrong!"

"Not so wrong when you are honored as a symbol, not a person. After all, God is both male and female, though the Roman church has forgotten the feminine part. Symbols evoke spiritual devotion in believers. They are a help for pilgrims in their journey to oneness with the Supreme."

" I shall think upon this. Is the Holy Grail hidden in that niche over there only a symbol as well?"

"Of course. But it is a powerful allegory of the inner journey."

"I begin to understand…. So then, John, you are my counterpart?"

"Yes, but only in a symbolic sense. Remember, even as a metaphor, for the sake of these people you must remain hidden too."

The girl in white had separated from the others now, and was climbing a ladder to the pentacle in the rock wall. She turned to face the group, grasping handholds on both sides. Settling her feet into recesses shaped for that purpose, she raised her head to touch the apex of the pentagram. Her outstretched hands, feet and head fit perfectly inside the shape of the recess. Her body formed a five-pointed star.

Raising her eyes to heaven, she allowed her spirit to rush past the Baptist and the Woman watching— past the confines of the cave, like a gust of wind sweeping through the forest below.

Her instructors, meanwhile, laid a white cloth bordered with gold upon a stone table. In the center was embroidered a circular emblem, bearing an Egyptian ankh, an eight-petaled flower and an equal-armed cross within its borders.

A smaller cloth, decorated with the image of a dove, was placed on one end of the table.

"They are preparing her for the Consolamentum," whispered John. "They will invoke the Holy Spirit to enter her body."

"Just as the Holy Spirit entered us in the Upper Room!" she remembered. "Did you know about that? Were you already dead?"

"Yes, I knew. The separation between your world and mine is thinner than you can realize."

At the moment her blue-robed initiators struck up a loud chanting, the woman's spirit came rushing back into her body. She was helped down from the pentagram, and escorted to the table. Four men lifted her onto the table, placing her head upon the dove-embroidered cloth. The woman in white appeared to remain in trance, totally relaxed, lying quietly upon the altar.

A gray haired man placed a stole, embroidered with two doves, around his neck. Approaching the table, he gestured gracefully back and forth with his hands, as if collecting energy between his palms.

The others began to softly sing tones in triads, placing their hands on the sides of the table, heads bowed.

At last the celebrant placed his palms upon the woman's head, leaving them there a long time. The toning increased in volume and pitch.

At a precise moment, all sound stopped. In the chamber reverberating with echoes, a bolt of light flew from high in the air, through the body of the priest, out his hands and into the head of the woman on the table.

Time stood still.

The figures in the cave appeared transfixed.

Nothing moved, until a dove rose, seemingly from nowhere, taking fluttering flight to the outside world.

At that signal, the woman sat up, to a great shout of welcome from the group. Two women helped her down from the table while two others placed a dark blue robe over her white vestments.

Singing, they filed out a different entrance from the one through which they had arrived, the new initiate leading their procession.

"Her life will never be the same," the Baptist said. "She died and was reborn at a higher level, closer to the Light of Truth.."

As the two disembodied spirits listened, the sound of singing faded slowly off into the distance.

AVE...Ave...Ave....

* * * * *

We hastened back to the car in the Montségur parking lot— not because we were in a hurry to leave that mysterious spot, but because we had to move fast in order to arrive at the Grotte de Niaux for our scheduled tour at 2:30 PM. Due to the fragile nature of the site, access is strictly controlled—a maximum of 11 visits a day, 20 people per visit, 45 minutes between each group. And you must sign up well in advance.

I remember my mother and father visiting the famous Lascaux Cave many years ago to view the beautiful prehistoric drawings one encounters in every art history book. I had always wanted to see them too; but the site, as most other similar ones, is now closed to the public. Body warmth and carbon dioxide exhaled by human beings altered the cave's atmosphere and damaged the paintings.

That's how really fragile the grotto environment is. Amazing, that those paintings lasted, untouched and unseen, for millennia. Nevertheless, there are still a few caves where people can view the beautiful drawings executed by paleolithic artists 13,000 years ago. The Grotte de Niaux is one of them.

Since Karol had wisely packed a picnic lunch in her backpack, hauling it up to the Montségur ruin and consuming it there, she was elected to be the driver. Heading west towards the town of Tarascon–sur-Ariège, she faultlessly swept us through winding river valleys between high hills, while we passed bread, cheese, fennel, olives and fruit back and forth between seats, eating greedily.

Obviously, I had regained my appetite, but the experience on the burning field still held me in its embrace. After the bountiful food had been consumed, I found myself looking dreamily out the window, losing myself in thought, while the rugged landscape rolled effortlessly by.

Meanwhile, Peter and Ross were having a conversation in the back seat. As we neared the beautiful Ariège River, I finally began to tune in. They were discussing caves and Cathars.

"Hi, guys, I'm back. Fill me in on what you were saying."

"Good thing one of us was paying attention to the road," Karol wisecracked. "Some navigator."

"Sorry. I'm still enthralled by that vision…. Karol, *Peter* is the navigator this trip, you know that!"

"Just trying to wake you up." She was chuckling.

"Turn south just ahead, after you cross the river," The navigator directed, picking up the cue. "We follow the Ariège down to Tarascon."

Ross caught me up on the back seat conversation. "Peter was telling us about the intricate cave system that underlies much of this area. How underground streams tunneling through the limestone that makes up much of southern France carve out caverns, which sometimes reach huge size."

"Yes," added Peter," and they were of great importance to the Cathars. The caves had always been places of initiation, but after the fall of Montségur, they became places of refuge as well. There were several in this area that figured significantly in Cathar history. A pity we don't have time to see them all!"

"Have to save something for the next trip," I piped up, only half kidding. "But Peter, please tell us about those sacred Cathar caves."

"Well, many people think Montségur was the end of the Cathars. But actually, they existed in lesser numbers for many generations. The believers went underground, literally as well as figuratively.

"Naturally, the Inquisition did not give up trying to annihilate them, picking on pockets of Cathars here and there. In at least two caves nearby, they just sealed them up and left them to die."

(Exclamations of horror and disbelief issued from all three of us.)

"Yes, they did," he nodded emphatically. "One of them was the cave of Lombrives, which is connected to Niaux. It was so large it was referred to as a cathedral. For two hundred years, Lombrives served as a meeting place and sacred retreat for Cathar faithful. It is even rumored that some of the treasure that was spirited away from Montségur was secreted there."

"So what happened?"

"In 1328, eighty-four years after the fall of Montségur, five hundred of the last Cathars who had taken refuge in the Cathedral Cave of Lombrives were walled in by the Senechal of Toulouse, by order of the Inquisition.

"They were forgotten until two hundred and fifty years later, when King Henry IV of France had the cave opened. They say skeletons lay in circles on the ground, hands and feet touching the ones next to them."

For a few moments, sitting there in the car, we mourned the fate of those poor people, each in our own way.

"Karol!" I suddenly remembered something.

"Do you remember when we went to Greece in October of 1994, and saw on TV in Athens that a group of Templars committed suicide in a burning farmhouse in France…or was it Switzerland?"

"Yes, I remember. What about it?"

"Well, they were found in the same position, dressed in ceremonial robes, laid out in a circle on the floor."

"That's right. Weird, isn't it?"

"Weird is right," from Ross. "The Cosmos works in mysterious whys."

"You mean 'ways'?"

"Right. Whys. That's what I said, isn't it?"

"Anyway," Peter continued, coming to Ross' rescue, "this seems to have become a pattern. In 1436, just over a hundred years later, the Inquisition sealed the caves south of Lombrives known as the Spougla de Bouan. This was a series of caves the Cathar remnant had fortified, ones that they had occupied for 3 centuries. Again, more than a hundred Cathars lost their lives."

"Their last hope. How sad." I felt devastated. My sensibilities were still razor sharp after the experience at Montségur."

"How sad? How *beastly!*" Ross fairly roared, getting red in the face. "Why has this all been covered up?"

Peter shook his head, raising his hands helplessly. "You have to look at who benefits from leaving it out of history. World history is full of worse, even, than the Inquisition, and much of it has not come to light."

"Until recently." Karol turned her head, glancing at the rest of us. "Many travesties have become public knowledge in the past 50 years. Like Stalin's purges and the Holocaust."

"True," confirmed Peter, "and more secrets are being revealed every moment.

155

He checked his watch. "Karol, we're near Tarascon-sur-Ariège. Let's all start looking for signs to the Grotte de Niaux. Time's getting short. Hope we make it by 2:30."

We passed through Tarascon-on-the-Ariège-River. Shortly afterwards, we found the sign pointing to the Cave. Turning off the highway, the road began climbing towards a sheer rock face set back against a mountain.

"There it is!" I pointed at a huge, rusty iron monument rather like the prow of a ship, guarding a hole in the cliff's face. As we came closer, we could see it enclosed an office and a viewing balcony. The whole massive edifice extended right into the mouth of the cavern.

We were not only on time, but a few minutes early, thanks to Karol's driving, Peter's navigation, and light traffic, so we sat on rocks in the parking lot, while Peter continued his lecture.

"There's one more cave I wanted to tell you about," he said. "This time, it's not a sad story. At least, not to my knowledge.

"Around Ussat, the sacred mountain of the Cathars, were many caverns utilized by the Sect. As with the others, these are not far from here, but most are inaccessible today. One of them, which it is possible to visit, is the Cave of Bethlehem, one of the cave-churches of the Ornolac group."

"What was so special about Bethlehem? And why the familiar name?"

Peter shrugged. "I don't know why they chose that name, although it may be because in a certain way it was a place of birth. It was a place of initiation. People who wanted to become 'Pures' would come there for very esoteric ceremonies culminating in the *Consolamentum,* the laying on of hands in which the Holy Spirit was believed to enter people and transform them."

"I wonder what the ceremonies consisted of?" Karol asked the question, but we all were curious to hear the answer.

"Nobody can tell for sure, but there are certain artifacts that give clues. Remaining there are a 'table' of rock supported by smaller stones, a granite altar, a square niche in the wall, and a man-sized pentagram cut into a wall. The telluric energies in that place are immense."

"How interesting!" I really would have like to have seen it, letting my imagination loose within the sacred space.

A trim, attractive, tourguide gathered us together, handing every other person a large lantern. We were instructed to pair off, sharing the light, and led into the great gaping black hole.

"This is like a birth canal into the womb of Mother Earth," I whispered to Karol, who nodded agreement. As we left the light of day behind, another dimensional reality drew us into its arms. I felt like Persephone entering the underworld in her annual winter descent.

Karol, holding the lantern in one hand, grasped mine with the other. The path was dangerous. Millennia of water, washing through, had sculpted the slippery wet limestone floor into bumps and hollows the size of washbasins or larger. With the lantern glancing off one thing then another in living light, now brightening a rise for us to surmount, now illuminating a black hollow to avoid, it seemed like something Disney would create— only this was frighteningly real.

Time became distorted. I have no idea how long we walked that hazardous pathway. Darkness everywhere, except the wavering beam of the lantern. Massive walls and ceiling deep below the surface of the earth enclosed us like a tomb.

Occasionally we stopped, while the guide explained some graffiti or cave lore in rapid French which, echoing off the walls and in a local accent, was very difficult to understand. She explained that although there were two galleries of paintings, the passageway to the one with red drawings had been closed off by an earthquake, so we would only be able to visit the gallery of black paintings.

"Oh gosh," Karol whispered to me, "an earthquake? Down here? Creepy!"

"That's all we would need," Ross whispered to Karol. "They would never know what happened to us back in Australia!"

Finally we reached a point where our guide instructed us to turn off all the lanterns. From now on, hers would be the only light. We were led into a wide spot in the tunnel, sort of moving shoulder to shoulder in the group, like sheep, so as to not be lost little lambs.

The guide shushed our murmuring, while making notes in an open book placed on a rock. It was necessary to record the time, the number of people in the group and the temperature. As I mentioned, the environment is very strictly monitored and controlled.

"Turn to your right and look over here," she directed, dramatically waving the beam of her lantern slowly across a panel of life sized animal drawings. "One of the finest examples of Magdalenian cave art."

"Magdalenian," I nudged the others. We were standing as close as possible, so as not to lose each other. "How about that for coincidence?"

The guide's light played slowly over first one drawing then another. Bison, deer, horses, antelopes manifested out of the darkness in turn, some superimposed, some alone on smooth sections of wall.

They were painted in black charcoal, probably mixed with fat or blood, according to the guide lady. And they were truly beautiful. More than beautiful—they were magical. And of course, that is the reason people think they were created, magic for a good hunt. But they were so artistically rendered! In places, small protrusions in the rock were incorporated into the form— perhaps a bump became an eye, or a nose. A swelling section delineated the curve of a stomach. These "primitive" people surely had observed the bodies of these animals with the eyes of the most professional artists!

Art, as shown before us in the representation of form on a two dimensional surface, is definitely nothing new. It is as old as mankind. It's in the DNA.

Here we were, encountering the work people created 13,000 years ago! Here was I, the artist, seeing firsthand the roots of my craft!

As my grandchildren would say, *"AWESOME!"*

After the carefully programmed time for observation, we followed our leader back through the slick corridors, twisting and turning, slipping and sliding out Mother Earth's birth canal to be reborn into the sunlight again.

"Born again," joked Peter as we emerged.

But I was thinking how graphically the experience would underscore the process of initiation. You enter the earth a seeker— you emerge filled with the Holy Spirit. There's a lot to be said for the journey.

It was my turn to drive back to LeThéron. We headed towards home. But there was one more stop we wanted to make on the way. Philippe, our host, had told us about a special church most visitors don't see. He said it was worth the effort.

And even as tired as we all were, from scaling mountains to trekking into the underworld, it certainly was.

The church in the tiny village of Vals was built on top of an ancient pagan shrine. It was easy to see why. From a small village square, the church rose against the hill behind it, seeming to grow out of huge, ancient boulders.

Beneath the church ran a tiny stream, in one side and out the other. If you mentally blanked out what human hands had constructed, what was left would have been a level enclosure surrounded by walls of native boulders, and the telluric energy of that stream gurgling underneath. A perfect place to dance in the moonlight. Or honor the Equinoxes and Solstices.

Entering the church through a passageway constructed in the crack between two of the gigantoliths (did I just coin that word?) we found ourselves in the body of the edifice. In front and on the sides were many levels and nooks. It reminded me vividly of what Montségur might have looked like when the inner structures were still intact.

159

"Say, Karol, doesn't this look like Montségur in its heyday—on a much smaller scale, of course?"

She scratched her head. "Maybe…yes…, guess I see what you mean."

Peter, Karol and I walked around checking out old tapestries, statues, etc., while Ross, as usual, was all over the place snapping pictures. Outside, we visited the adjacent cemetery and traced the little stream to where it entered and left under the building. Ross gathered some water for his collection.

You know, one would have thought that with all the activities and emotions of the day there would be very little energy left to appreciate this small church. But the truth was, the site had so much energy of its own, we were revived, and able to proceed home by way of small country roads— to yet another pick-up gourmet feast orchestrated by Ross and myself.

This time it was pasta with truffle sauce and fresh green salad, grapes, nuts, some more excellent local wine, with a bit of chocolate to top it all off.

Such a day it had been! Consider—we had climbed to the sky, to the Noah's ark of Montségur, descended into the bowels of the earth at the Grotte de Niaux, and visited a small but special church incorporating the powerful energies of earth's surface, on which we live. It was like a shaman's journey to all three realms.

Tomorrow, we decided, we would take it a little easier. No long drives, no major historic monuments. Philippe and Margaret suggested an interesting town nearby, built in a circle. They call it *Aigne,* the snail, because of its spiral streets.

That sounded nice and relaxed. A day without stress and big emotion!

Yes. It really sounded relaxing.

But it wasn't.

Because unknown to me, in the heart of the snail I was about to stumble upon the meaning of my vision.

160

Chapter Sixteen

DANCING IN THE FLAMES

* * * * *

As the singing faded, a new sound rose to replace it. Measured, regular footsteps, the clank of metal against metal—surely an army must be approaching!

Together, the disembodied witnesses rushed outside the Cave of Initiation, spying two different groups of people on the path below the cliffs.

One, the Good Men and Women, walking peacefully along; the other a small band of soldiers, running, pursuing them, swords drawn. Instantly, the moment the religious group perceived the soldiers, they scurried towards a crack in the cliff face, disappearing inside just as the troops were about to catch up to them.

"Have no fear," the John Essence comforted the woman. "They know these caverns well. These people will never be found by the Inquisition's men. Unfortunately, others will not be so lucky in times to come. Because they will not obey the Roman church, they will be hunted down, besieged, put to the sword and cast into great fires."

"My heart is heavy to know this, for they follow the true Way taught by the Master. His words, through me, have brought this fate upon them.

"For this, I grieve."

"Sister, it is not because of you. It is the perversity of humankind that has created this division among the Faithful. Follow them if you so desire. You may enter their refuge."

She willed herself through the crack into a great cavern, so huge that hundreds of people could easily gather inside. The group she had followed was sitting by a beautiful subterranean lake, praying silently. She saw their reflections in the water's shiny black surface, lit by torches they had apparently cached in their secret cathedral.

Could I see myself in this watery mirror? she wondered. Hovering over the lake, she perceived only the reflection of a soft purple ball of light.

This must be my life force, the essence of my True Self, she decided, watching it gently pulse on the surface of the water. Slowly, another ball of light brightened next to her own. It was white, not purple.

"Who are you?" she asked the white light, without fear. For she became less amazed each time a miraculous event occurred.

"It is I, yourself," came the puzzling answer.

"How can this be?"

"We are one stream, divided into two," the beautiful voice replied. "You are the Dark Madonna, I am the Light Madonna. You shall remain hidden until the world is ready. I shall be seen and revered openly as the mother of God, but we are both aspects of the Holy Feminine.

"We shall be united and restored to our rightful place beside our consort one day, after a great cleansing has occurred.

"Come, enter the water with me. Become the underground stream. Flow into the future, until the time of Restoration."

If anyone present had been watching instead of praying, they might have seen two balls of softly pulsing light dive into the lake, disappearing beneath its waters.

162

* * * * *

The next morning started ordinarily enough. We slept late, ate a leisurely breakfast, did a little laundry and hung it to dry by the almond tree.

It wasn't until nearly lunchtime that Ross drove us to Olonzac to buy bread, and on to the village of Aigne, pronounced EN-yuh, the "snail." Margaret remembered an interesting stone cutter, and an icon painter there. "Well worth a visit," she said.

It was interesting indeed.

Just outside the walls of the inner village, a curious sight brought us to a stop. "This must be the place," remarked Karol, as Ross parked the car. From a stone house on the corner of the Rue d'Occitanie, grotesquely sculpted faces peered at us, emerging from the building stones themselves.

Someone had chipped off the stucco covering, all around the front door and along one wall, chiseling fantastic faces and forms into the building rocks underneath. (Or perhaps, as some sculptors believe, the forms had been living in the stone, waiting to be freed.)

A mysteriously smiling fish poked its head out from the wall at the corner of the lintel, as if it were guardian of the portal. Below it, bordering the door, climbed a gargoyle-like bird, surmounting two grimacing masks. The upper face looked like a Mayan deity; the lower seemed Jovian in style. The other side of the door had been carved in the same manner, into fantastic animal shapes and primitive human forms. Some were so imaginary we could not even begin to identify them.

Along the front wall two related figures, rising waist high from waves like King and Queen of the Waters, caught my eye. She, bare breasted, with flowing hair, gestured gracefully towards her partner, who was separated from her by a fanciful sea creature resembling a whale. He, squat and square, wild of hair and beard,

163

gestured back. They looked straight out at us, daring us to name them.

A marine Adam and Eve? Neptune and a mermaid? Lord and Lady of Aigne rising from the waters?

"King Arthur and Queen Guinevere!" suggested Ross, wryly grinning.

"Hardly," Karol laughed. "Let's go inside."

Peter's knock on the wooden door brought a tall, thin man to greet us. He wore faded jeans, well saturated with stone dust, and an equally faded lavender T-shirt. He was wiping his mouth with the back of his hand.

"Entrez," he gestured dourly towards the interior of his house. Stepping down into the dimly lit interior, we filed inside.

We had surprised him at lunch. A woman and small child were sitting by a table upon which lay the remains of bread, cheese and a bottle of wine. He swept the food scraps away to the kitchen rather awkwardly, while the woman quickly left in a rustle of skirts, carrying the wide-eyed child in her arms.

"We apologize for disturbing you," Peter said in his excellent French.

"Mais ça ne fait rien," mumbled the sculptor, "No problemme." We presumed that was English.

The room was filled with amazing sculptures. A lot of fish and more free-standing fantastic figures. Many were large; all were interesting. I looked for something small to buy, for I could hardly carry, or even ship, the heavy pieces. There didn't seem to be anything weighing less than twenty pounds.

Meanwhile, Peter was conversing with the man, whose name was Pascal. He explained that this was a house inherited from his father. Pascal lived elsewhere, but he was attempting to turn the building itself into an artform. The tourists seem to like it, he said, although with a shrug of his narrow shoulders he indicated that not many buy.

"They are too large to carry away," I explained. "I wanted to find something small." He simply raised his shoulders

164

expressively. The man did a lot of shrugging, but then again, I thought, perhaps he was just shy—or just resigned.

I did find a sculpture of two fish that interested me, because I am a Pisces—but again, too large. Drat! Karol and I continued browsing among the figures.

Meanwhile, Ross had emptied a cache of small stones from his knapsack onto the ground by the front door. He was showing each treasure to Pascal, who was sitting on the step, examining every stone with interest.

"This is an Aborigine Healing Rock." Ross was holding a small, round white pebble in his hand. "I collect round stones of every color, but I don't have a green one."

Peter looked on with interest. Karol and I joined them just as Ross held it out to Pascal. "Do you feel anything special from it?" he asked the sculptor, who, after all, feels lots of stones of many different kinds. If it felt different, he should be the person to know.

Pascal raised his shoulders again, but his face took on new animation. Ross had somehow forged a link between them. A shared love of stones had breached his shyness and bridged the language barrier.

"Ross," I remarked, "That backpack must weigh a ton, what with the rocks you carry, and the water!" Good thing he is young and strong. After he had replaced his treasures, Ross hoisted the knapsack on his shoulder as if it were filled with feathers.

We prepared to leave. But Pascal had disappeared into the house. He emerged, pressing a small stone, carved on one edge with the face of a woman, into my hand.

"Merci, monsieur," I thanked him, asking him how much he wanted for it.

"Rien, nothing. It is only a pebble." He steadfastly refused payment of any kind, but I went inside and left a few francs on his table before we said goodbye.

"What an interesting man," I remarked, fondling the carved pebble, warm in my hand, as we began walking down the circular street leading to the village center.

We had not gone more than a hundred yards when Pascal came running up, depositing an egg-shaped polished green stone into Ross' hand. Ross, astonished, was ecstatic, thanking the man profusely.

We said goodbye a second time, this time with even warmer hearts.

A bit further down the circular corridor, we came upon a herd of cats.

What do you call a big bunch of cats? A pod? A gaggle? A pack? I guess you just say a big bunch of cats, so numerous that, moving, we found it hard to count them.

"How many do you get, Karol? I think there are eighteen."

"I quit at 20, counting the kitten."

He really should have only counted for less than half, since the little Tabby was so tiny he looked like he should not have left his mother.

The men and Karol walked on ahead, while I spent about ten minutes trying to take photographs of the cat clan. Suddenly, they jumped from their positions on windowsills, rocks, and potted plants towards a woman with impossibly red hair who, emerging from a door, held a bag of Friskies in her hands.

Feeding time!

A blur of fur descended upon the pans the woman filled. Munching and purring resounded in the corridor. I asked if the kitten had a mother here. She said no; it just appeared a few days before, from nowhere.

It was a spectacle to behold, all those kitties in feeding frenzy. Photos could not do the scene justice. I was just happy someone was taking care of them.

By the time I caught up to the others, they had arrived at the studio of the icon painter, a woman, and were already deep in conversation. There must have been some kind of instantaneous bonding going on; for, as I stepped down into the gallery room, the painter had Karol's head in both hands, and was looking deep into her eyes.

"You must know, you are following the right path," she was telling Karol emphatically. "Do not fear. God is looking out for you. You will be all right."

Karol's eyes were filled with tears.

"Be sure, you are doing what is right," she repeated emphatically, her face only inches away from Karol's. "You must trust yourself. God will guide you!"

She drew Karol into her arms, encircling her with love. Karol was weeping openly. Obviously, emotions in that studio were running high.

"You see," and this time her glance took in all four of us as she released Karol from her grasp, "I know who you are. I recognized you immediately! I knew, this morning, when I awakened, you would be coming. I was waiting for you to appear on my doorstep."

It felt like we had entered my grandmother's house for Thanksgiving dinner. Such a welcome! *But how could she have known?*

In the few minutes before my arrival, somehow a connection to the Cathar energy had been established between the artist and my friends. It was like we had all been together before, in blue Cathar robes. The feeling was surreal, and very very strong.

The icon painter introduced herself as Françoise. "I must go to fetch my husband," she said. "He must meet you too."

While she was away, we looked around at the artwork on her walls. Most of the paintings were icons, done in the traditional manner. Sacred paintings of haloed Madonnas and Saints. But a few were pleasant watercolors of landscapes and flowers.

Shortly, Françoise reappeared with her husband, introducing him all around. The men, Françoise and Karol fell into animated conversation.

167

But I felt drawn a bit apart, for some reason, and wandered over to a table upon which lay the artist's portfolio.

I began to idly leaf through its contents of unframed artwork.

Suddenly, as I turned a painting over, my knees felt weak.

There, looking straight up at me from the paper was a woman, dressed in a blue robe, standing amid flames, which were rising to consume her. Above her head, what was unmistakably her soul— in the form of a dove— ascended, surrounded by shimmering rainbow waves of light, toward the heavens.

I must have gasped.

The group fell silent, looking at me.

"This is my vision!" I cried, holding up the painting.

Then, overcome with emotion, I sank limply to the floor.

Chapter Seventeen

Web of Connection

* * * * *

Side by side, the two small fuzzy balls of pulsing light, one violet, one white, floated along in the underground stream. It seemed the river led into the future, for as they moved gently along, they entered realms of experiences yet unknown.

Soon, they flowed into a great space, which appeared to be a limitless hidden cavern. It enveloped them in a warm darkness filled with tiny, flickering lights attached to nearly imperceptible, moving strands of pure energy.

They seemed to have no control over their path through this etheric forest. Surprisingly, whenever they brushed against one of the lights, an unfamiliar scene enlarged into reality. The moment they touched it, they were drawn into the scene. The moment they withdrew, the scene faded back into a simple spark.

Thus, they entered the world of a city near a huge arm of the ocean. Horses, drawing carriages filled with goods and people, moved along streets between many buildings, which people appeared to inhabit. The houses were much different from the simple, one-story dwellings familiar to the observing pair. These houses were higher, and far more densely populated.

As they watched in horror, the earth below the city began to tremble, then shake like a dog tossing water from its fur. Buildings collapsed upon carriages and people. A great wailing arose from the rubble, as walls of fire advanced to consume the city.

169

Next, they touched upon a scene of war. Men in trenches screamed in agony as toxic gases tore out their insides and blinded their eyes. At the same time, uniformed men in a secret room pushed tiny toy soldiers across a diagram, like children playing a game of pebbles in the sand.

They moved on to a beautiful prairie, filled with waving grasses and flowers. In cultivated fields, crops grew, nodding in the breeze. Before their unseen eyes, the grasses and crops and flowers began to wither and die, shriveling into dust.

The twin spirits next encountered another scene of war. This time, huge droning machines flew in the air, from which explosives fell on the countryside below. One particular machine passed over a large city, dropping something that turned the entire city into ashes in less than an instant. There was no wailing this time.

There was nobody left to cry.

On they floated, on the underground river, approaching one spark in the darkness after another. Each revealed a scene of terror and destruction.

Women were raped and burned as witches. People who did not profess the dominant religion were tortured and killed.

Greedy politicians sacrificed human lives to win territory and power. Animals were abused, starved, killed and eaten.

Fishing boats, dragging huge nets, destroyed all the life caught in their webs, depopulating the oceans. Farmers, thinking to improve their crops, poured toxic chemicals upon them, poisoning the food and water. Huge places of manufacturing dumped noxious waste materials into lakes and rivers, and blew clouds of toxins into the air.

People tortured and killed other people, just because they were different from themselves. Hate seemed to be winning over Love. People crying, people dying, children starving because of famine produced by mankind's own greed.

170

Great plagues of sickness wiped out whole cities and villages. Earthquakes and tidal waves decimated more. The two small balls of pulsating light absorbed sadness to the point of saturation.

Was there no hope left?

Would there not be any healing?

At the deepest moment of their despair for the earth and all its peoples, hope returned. The two feminine Beings saw the earth begin to shake off its mantle of pollution.

Floods washed the soil clean again, continents rose from the oceans, as others submerged, carrying their chaos beneath the waters. Fires destroyed the sources of toxicity, leaving rich ashes to fertilize a new land. The fields began to bloom again, the forests to stand tall. Animals returned, and prospered.

But what of mankind?

With pleasure, the unseen twins encountered a remnant of people in every realm, moving forward with new respect for each other and the earth which supports them.

In this new world, everything seemed changed. Old institutions based on greed and envy and evil were replaced with new ones based on cooperation and sharing. The people appeared to have been blessed at last with enduring peace and prosperity.

"They have come to understand the Truth," the Purple One observed to the White, as they finally moved through the forest of twinkling realms, back into the dark tunnel of the underground stream.

Ahead of them, daylight illuminated the river, bubbling to the surface. The pair of feminine Energies fused into one form as they burst up through the waters. The woman stood alone where they had emerged as two, on the edge of a spring, complete in her own body once more.

She looked around, puzzled to discover she was situated next to the very spring that flowed from her mountain,

171

in the forest below her cave. And Yeshua had appeared, standing so close, she could feel his warmth.

Oh! How she longed to touch him! But this time she knew it was too soon. To comfort herself, she felt the reality of the gold ring upon her finger, the token of his promise to be with her always.

Together, they began to walk up the path to her abode.

"Have you seen the future?" he asked, knowing full well that she had. "Do you understand your part in it?"

"Yes," she answered to the first part. But to the second, she shook her head in bewilderment. "In what way am I to be a part of all of this?"

"YOU SHALL BE THE HOPE OF MANKIND," he answered. "This is your final task. It is for you to comprehend."

Having thus announced her mission, he vanished.

She was alone again, a small figure climbing the path to her retreat, pondering upon the meaning of his words.

* * * * *

Hands reached out to support me as I sagged to the cool, stone floor, still holding THE PAINTING up as if for God to see.

The same hands sustained me lovingly, as consciousness rushed back. Opening my eyes, I found myself staring into the compassionate face of Françoise.

"C'est bien," I croaked weakly. Repeating, in a stronger— although rather embarrassed— voice, "It's OK."

"Oui, c'est bien," responded Françoise. "It is natural, when one encounters oneself, to be overcome by emotion." She took me by the arms, assisting me to rise.

"But how did you know my vision, to paint it?" I persisted, seated in the chair to which Françoise had led me, slowly regaining my composure.

Françoise smiled knowingly. "I, too, have seen it," she declared. "I, also, was there!"

She gestured at the painting Karol had rescued and replaced upon the table. "You must always remember this: she is not standing in the flames, she is *dancing* in them."

Turning her attention back to the group gathered protectively around me, Françoise added, "We were all there. You arrived in my studio because it is important for you to know this: we are all strongly connected through that shared experience. In my waking meditation I saw you this morning, and I knew you would be coming to find us."

"I don't really understand, but I do believe you." I was trying to get a grip on the fullness of this slippery concept of *connection*; but although I was experiencing gentle, sparkling touches from its realm, in that moment I could perceive *connection* only in fuzzy shades of gray.

Ross moved to the center of the studio to pour some of his sacred water on the floor. With the liquid, he formed an equal armed cross upon the gray flagstone.

"Yes, perfect," observed Peter. "We should celebrate our connections."

The six of us formed a circle around the cross of water, holding hands, in silent prayer, rejoicing, ending with the traditional Cathar greeting. The room's temperature actually became warmer from the energy we created.

Of course, to complete the celebration, we had to take pictures, and partake of a little wine and cheese. Is not sharing food the most ancient ritual? You may have noticed I mention food a lot. In my family, it is very nearly a sacrament.

Karol discovered a Medieval-looking fish print in the portfolio. Holding it so we all could see, she begged, "Tell us what it means."

"It contains hidden Cathar doctrine," Françoise responded, taking the print from Karol to point out its details. "You see, it was dangerous to write about their beliefs, so the Cathars encoded them in drawings." She traced the outline of the design with a delicate finger.

"Yes, it is a fish, but a special variety of fish called a *dorade*. This is a play on the word *adorer*, which means 'to adore,' and it refers to the adoration of Mary Magdalene, whom they could not openly worship. It is also a reference to the statue of a much venerated Black Madonna called 'La Daurade' which presently is kept in a church in Toulouse."

"The Magdalene."

She nodded. "Of course."

"These marks around the fish represent past lives, stages of enlightenment, and perfection. The red and black lines surrounding the fish represent our journey back to the Light; and the black half cross on the border shows that we must remain hidden, revealing no more than half of our beliefs to the world."

"What do those other symbols mean?" Karol was referring to cryptic letters in boxes surrounding the fish.

"I have added some automatic writing, which says in effect: *Now is the time to shout out what God is telling us.*"

The rest of us murmured assent. In our hearts we were already shouting.

It was time to leave Aigne, but before leaving, Karol and Ross each bought a copy of the *Dorade*.

Karol saw that I was yearning over the painting of my vision at Montségur.

"You need to have this, Cinnie," she remarked, handing it to me. "Merry Christmas, friend!"

As I sit in my studio writing this manuscript, the Lady in Blue, dancing in the flames, smiles sweetly at me from her place on the wall above my computer. I think she's the spirit of the Magdalene too, encouraging me.

It had been a short but emotional day. On the way home, we decided not to go out to dinner, but rather to eat up provisions on hand, since Peter and Ross were to depart the following morning, and Karol and I the day after. So Ross and I concocted our last gourmet vegetarian meal to share. A sort of "Last Supper."

But instead of a *Seder,* it was a feast of rosemary/garlic potatoes, Brussels sprouts with leeks and lemon, canned tomatoes for color, and rice enriched with sautéed celery and garlic. Wonderful *pain de campagne,* dipped in olive oil and local wine topped off the feast. All from leftovers. Now that's truly creative!

"So what was the deeper meaning of the painting?" I asked Peter, who was settling down on a couch after dinner and dishes. Ross was tiptoeing around the garden outside, recording the night sounds of frogs and crickets on his little tape recorder.

"Peter, I know we are all connected, but what does that *really* mean?"

"It's the way the Cosmos works," he answered, not very helpfully. "You'll have to meditate on it."

"No short cuts?"

"Afraid not. People have to discover it themselves."

"Darn. Well, guess I'll have to go upstairs and try."

It was hard to say goodnight, knowing we would be parting in the morning. But there was comfort in the fact we would remain friends, with many wonderful shared experiences, always.

Later, nestled in my bed, looking out the small, square window at a star-studded sky, I earnestly pleaded to be shown the meaning of *connectedness.*

With closed eyes, I saw myself at night, atop the highest mountain in the world, staring into the heavens. All the stars spread out in the sky above me.

They were beautiful.

Then, whether I had drifted into sleep, I know not— but the scene subtly changed around me. I no longer felt solid rock beneath my feet, but floated, surrounded by stars above, beside and below.

It was as if I were drifting in some endless, limitless black void.

175

But the void was not empty. I could feel the movement of almost invisible strands, gossamer spider webs, extending in all directions, waving and undulating like stems of kelp in the embrace of an ocean current. They pervaded the limitless space with motion, and soft, fluttering sound.

And I floated freely, unhindered by the web through which I moved.

Along each of the ker-trillions of strands, glowed tiny points of light. Oddly, although they sparkled, they did not reflect into the soft darkness around them. Each point of light was unique, complete unto itself, yet connected to all the others by the waving etheric web. What strange void had I entered?

Curious, I focused my attention on one at random. To my amazement, my attention created a beam much like that of a flashlight, which played upon the tiny point of light, magnifying it as through the lens of a microscope.

There, as if I were present in the scene, I saw a husband and wife drinking morning coffee. She was screaming awful words at him, from some deep anger. He slammed his newspaper down on the table, turning to slap her face.

I shuddered, quickly withdrawing my attention from the scene.

Next, I chose another point of light to focus upon. It revealed a yellow flower in a field, opening to the sun. Here, I lingered a moment or two, enjoying its beauty, before moving my attention beam to another tiny sparkle.

This time I watched a wounded Roman soldier being brought home to his mother on a litter. I felt her heart break, as she took him into her arms, bathing his young face with her tears.

Some of the dewdrops revealed the future, some the past, others the present—and it was as if I became a part of every scene.

One point of light illuminated a simple thought—a solution to an equation. Another showed me a Good Samaritan ministering to a homeless woman. Everywhere I fixed the beam of my

176

conscious attention, I discovered the lens of my perception revealing every thought, word, emotion, deed ever created, feeling them all as if they were my own.

Everything was there! Each tiny spark of light contained a little world!

What if...I thought...*What if some other soul shined her light of awareness on the same little dewdrop as I did? We would experience the same thing! Perhaps Françoise and I both saw a Blue Lady dancing in the flames!*

But, what if people see something that does not fit with their sense of who they are, or how the world works?

Well, I considered— *they must just turn away and refuse to let it in!*

We choose!

Aha!

I became conscious of a great Light far off, towards what must be the center of this vast space. It seemed to draw me towards it as if on an invisible path, spiraling around in the forest of tiny points of brightness. This Light is White, Hot and Welcoming. I feel its warm Love reaching out to me.

But I know it will be a long time until I arrive there. I sense many others moving along the same path towards the Star— or is it a Sun? at the center.

I know now everything can manifest inside this cosmic realm of infinite possibilities—good and evil, love and hate. But they are all parts of the Whole, all drops of energy stuck on the moving, waving, etheric threads that fill this Void in which our souls exist.

There is no Father God, sitting on a throne! There is no Satan with Devil horns and pitchfork—unless one wishes to perceive them as such! There is only what *can* be, what you can create with your own awareness, by your own choices.

Big Aha!

Everything is part of this web of *connection.* And everyONE!

CAUNES MINERVOIS,
Notre Dame du Cros:
Marriage of the Virgin

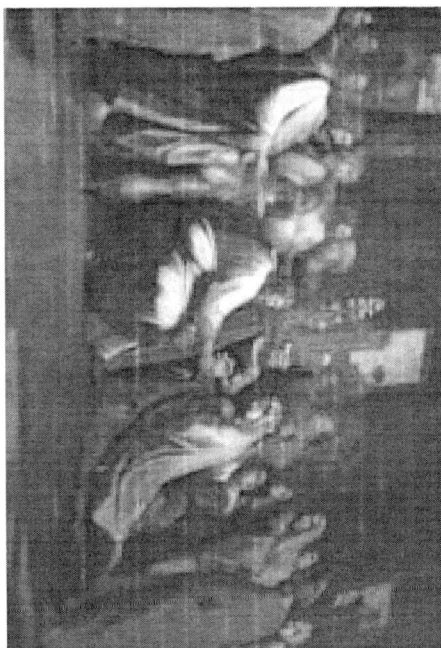

Chapter Eighteen

WEDDING ON THE WALL

* * * * *

I shall be the hope of mankind...I shall be the hope of mankind...I shall be the hope of mankind...I shall be the hope of mankind....

Words in her mind echoed the rhythmic pace of her footsteps, climbing the familiar path towards her cave. As the terrain grew steeper, the cadence changed, slowing to a simpler beat—Why me?...why me?...why me?....

Exhausted beyond measure, she sank down upon the meditation rock by its entrance, leaning against the cool wall behind it. But even with her body at rest, her mind could not be stilled. So many new experiences, mysterious miracles, unfathomable questions!

After a long time, the needs of her person overshadowed the chaos of her thoughts. Right there, sitting upon her rock, she fell into deep slumber.

When she awoke, long afternoon shadows cast by the mountain were creeping across the forest below, extinguishing bright green tree tops, line by line.

She shivered, arose and entered the cavern to fetch a piece of cloth against the chill. Catching sight of some bread left by James—how long ago?—she abruptly became aware of the emptiness in her stomach.

"If I am to be the hope of mankind," she giggled, looking down at her thin body, "I suppose it would be well if I were to eat!"

Surprisingly, the bread and water did not satisfy her. Until this moment, she had very often forgotten food entirely. But now, energy rising within her body demanded nourishment.

As if in answer to her desires, old friend Maximim puffed up to the entrance with a heavily laden donkey leashed behind him.

"Ah, Maximum! It is well that you have come!" She ran to greet him with a kiss on both plump cheeks and a loving look into his eyes.

"Dear Lady!"

"But why is your beast so heavy burdened? Are we to have a feast for all the angels?"

He laughed briefly at her gentle jest. "No, I met James, the Joseph, in the village. He told me to prepare much food and bring it to you; for he intends to gather many of your friends and followers to join you anon. He said it may be the last…." Her friend bit off his words. His heart wished mightily he could bring them back again.

"Last…time?" She knew what he was going to say. "Perhaps you are right, dear Maximim. But I have no fear of dying, and strangely enough, right now I am beginning to feel life rising within me!"

"Let us then nourish it." So saying, he unloaded the bundles of food, laying them tidily upon the stone floor. Each time he bent, the brown hood flopped to cover his tonsured head. When he stood again, it bobbed back into place. Absurdly, the sight of this impromptu dance of the hood amused her.

"Will you not join me in partaking of some of this bounty?" she invited him as soon as he had finished, politely restraining her giggles.

"No, dear friend, I must return before night overtakes us in the forest. The woods are eerie at night. I fear unseen spirits and evildoers." Maximim nervously pulled the cloak

closer around his corpulent figure, as if to ward off sinister ghosts.

"Return, then, if you must, but will you come back tomorrow? Tonight I shall weave a spell over the forest so that all manner of evil will depart, and you will have naught to fear."

He looked at her quizzically. This teasing jesting was something new. Was everything really well with her?

"I am perfectly fine, my dear Maximim," she read his thoughts again. "I am done with sadness. It has had too much of a hold over me since Yeshua left my life."

"You know he has never really left." Her friend thought to soothe her.

"Nobody knows that more that I," she responded cryptically, the gleam of a twinkle in her eyes. She threw back the mane of auburn hair jauntily.

"How so?" He was puzzled at her strange behavior.

"I shall tell you upon your return. Perhaps it will bring you back the sooner."

"As you wish, dear Lady."

And wondering what had come over his long-time friend, Maximim hastily left for the village below.

Gleefully, she opened the bundles, exposing their treasures one by one. Bread, nuts, figs, dates, honey in the comb, sweet cakes…she fell upon them hungrily.

Sated at last, the woman sat upon her bed wiping crumbs from her mouth, remembering another feast— one at which she had shared with Yeshua. It was the feast of their second marriage.

How proudly he had presented her as his wife! How lovingly his dark eyes had softened as their gaze swept down to her womb, swollen with the fruit of their betrothal!

She had reached up to touch the crown of flowers encircling his head. His hair had still been moist and fragrant from the spikenard of her anointing.

181

And before Martha, and Lazarus, and God and all the others, he had bent down and kissed her lips, full of passion and desire.

She had blushed then, and she blushed now, as she sat still upon the bed of furs, playing with the golden ring upon her finger, remembering.

* * * * *

Peter and Ross left the next morning, to spend some time at the Château of Castelfranc, and move on with their own journeys.

Castelfranc is a historic monument in the center of Cathar Country. The château there has been used for the past several years by the Heart to Peace Foundation, as a place where groups of young people from war-torn Bosnia are brought for rest and recreation.

It was set up as a reconnection with the ancient Bogomil energy that established Catharism in Southwest France—a contemporary manifestation of Cathar principles, so to speak.

At breakfast, before their departure, I told them about my meditation, or dream, or whatever it was. Karol, nodding wisely between sips of coffee, summed up the whole complicated idea in a thimble.

"It's sort of like the Internet," said she. "There's all that information out there, but you don't connect with it until you pull it up with your Internet Browser."

Now why couldn't I have thought of that?

After reluctant good-byes, the two of us sadly watched the Peugeot bearing Ross and Peter pull away from LeThéron, heading down the dusty road towards Siran. It had been a week of very important discoveries, and much sharing. All of us had come away from these experiences with new understanding.

We had changed a bit. No matter where our lives would subsequently lead, none of us would ever be quite the same as before our days together.

But Karol and I still had our own journey to make, away from the turmoil of Cathar history. This next week of our sojourn in France was to be a different foray—a woman's pilgrimage, into the heart of the Magdalene.

However, before moving forward into phase II, one more day remained at LeThéron. Since Margaret had suggested some local places of interest to visit, we two female adventurers of a certain age turned the trusty green Renault's nose towards a circle of nearby Churches.

The first one we discovered was the small Romanesque church of St. Germain, standing alone and lonely in a forest clearing. Empty, but in pristine condition, it was easy to imagine the stone walls enclosing a congregation of Christians of the time, far removed from tumult of the Albigensian Crusade.

Yet, interestingly, we found traces of Heresy, even there. A window in the shape of a Cathar cross, admitted light into the church's vacant nave. On the outside, another Cathar cross formed a half chipped away boss. Some ancient graffiti perpetrator had inscribed a pentagram containing a circle, on one of the decorative stone arches hugging the rounded exterior wall.

The church at Pépieux, (yes, PÉPIEUX!) was far different. Constructed and reconstructed over centuries, it was much larger and more ornate. In its reincarnation as a living church, it was complete with congregation and Masses, bulletin board, hymnals, holy water, statues of Bernadette at Lourdes and St. Martha, among the customary others.

But even there, in blood red color, on the columns and, in particular, the back of the pulpit for all to see—the Cathar Cross! Four equal arms, flared at the ends.

We were to observe these same crosses in every church we visited in Languedoc.

Why? These are not the crosses of crucifixion upon which Jesus is said to have suffered, the Christian symbol.

Are they secret reminders for those whose eyes are sufficiently unveiled to recognize the sign? Are they traces of the old Christian religion once dominating this region? The old religion that so many clung to and died for?

How many hidden symbols still encode the secrets? Is that ancient religion still alive in the hearts of the people?

We began to perceive these signs with new awareness.

And it was with that same new awareness that I regarded a gigantic painting framed in red marble, on a wall in the church of Notre Dame du Cros (Our Lady of the Cross), near Caunes-Minervois.

"Karol, you have to look at this!" I called excitedly to my long-suffering friend who, by now, was getting used to my sudden expeditions into speculation. She hastened up the aisle to where I was standing, near the altar, gazing upwards as raptly as Bernadette must have stood contemplating the Blessed Virgin's apparition at Lourdes.

"This painting is called 'The Marriage of the Virgin' Karol, but I think it really is the marriage of Mary Magdalene and Jesus!"

"Why do you say that?"

"Look at the clues! The "Joseph" in the painting is much too young to be the father of Jesus. And he's holding a blooming staff in his hand."

"Yes, I see what you are saying," she agreed. "He does look awfully young… no gray hair... and we saw the blooming staff in connection with Mary Magdalene before, in Rennes-le – Château.

"But that blooming staff could also refer to Joseph's carrying on the seed of the House of David, couldn't it?"

"By that you mean Jesus? Right, but in that case it would be support for the theory he was Jesus' natural father."

"Hmmm."

"And look what else. The bride is wearing the red robe and black cloak of Isis!"

"Hmmm!" This time with rising and falling inflection, more like "Maybe so!"

Karol took out the little binoculars she carried in her backpack, scanning the painting to catch more detail.

"See the other symbols?" I prompted. "That fellow on the left is carrying a jar, and a basin…"

"For anointing?"

"Sure. That was part of the marriage ceremony."

"I remember Mary Magdalene anointed Jesus just before he went into Jerusalem for the last time," she recalled. "Could that have been a marriage?"

"Very possible. Remind me to tell you what I have read about Dynastic Marriage among the Jews of that time."

"Dynastic marriage?"

"Yes, the marriage of people carrying on the dynasty of the kingly line."

"OK, tell me about it when we're driving back to LeThéron."

"Sure. But look, there's other clues in this painting."

"What more?"

"Notice the people making special gestures. That finger pointing upwards is supposed to refer to John the Baptist, though I can't figure why he's represented here. Secret societies have special gestures. I'm sure there are lots of other clues that I don't know enough to understand yet.

"But there's one more I *do* understand, a real kicker! Look carefully behind the bride's cloak. See the baby?"

"Oh, wow, I didn't notice it before."

"According to the code of dynastic marriage, the final wedding ceremony could not take place until after the bride was at least three months pregnant."

"To ensure continuation of the line, I suppose. That would make sense."

The two of us stood looking, and photographing, the amazing painting, before finally leaving the church to explore the setting in which it stood.

Founded around 900 CE, the church had been built as a place of pilgrimage on land that had always been sacred. From a cleft between high cliffs, now dotted with pitons for the pleasure of rock climbers, issues a clear stream, running merrily year round. The stream provides water for irrigating its alluvial terrace, where crops are grown. Bordering it rises a forest, sheltering stone shrines and hermitages. A natural oasis, a fitting environment for honoring the feminine spirit.

Ave Maria, I thought, seeing the entwined A and M within a circle on the church's exterior wall. *Yes, Hail to you, Mary. You healed me, and you brought me here to learn who you really are. It is your time, now. Your time to be restored to balance with the Holy Masculine.*

Holy Feminine, half of God—Ave Maria!

…And it is fitting you are honored here as Our Lady of the Cross.

But whose Cross do they mean?

Chapter Nineteen

DYNASTIC MARRIAGE

******

She settled back among the furs, transposing memories into dreams, while stars traveled across the night sky, once again melting into morning's light.

Opening her eyes, the woman on the bed stretched languidly, an unaccustomed feeling of power rising through her body. Was it the full meal? Perhaps the telluric energy of earth, coursing through the rock which surrounded her? Or was it something different, something new?

She pondered a while, trying to analyze the source of this fresh sense of energy, sense of purpose.

Purpose! That was it! At last she felt aligned with her purpose. Up until this moment, she had sought her life's purpose... performed it blindly...struggled with it... tried to analyze it...resisted it...retreated from it. For the first time she felt it coursing through her body, her life, without resistance.

Although everything was far from clarified, she felt as if a cosmic river was running right through her, and she, floating easily within its flow, had been relieved of all obstacles.

Exhilarated, she ran lightly to the cave's entrance, crying greetings to the sun, the sky, the earth, the trees, the rocks, the animals. New Life! She felt New Life!

Gaily, almost giddily, she snatched an empty jar, and tripped down the path to draw water from the spring. Having filled the jar with its cold, clear liquid, she sat for a moment, resting beside the pool, among mossy stones.

Reflections of the sky and trees played upon its placid surface. How beautiful, those ripples moving out in circles from pebbles tossed into its depths! They seemed to carry her back into the waiting world of memory.

In those fractured reflections, she fancied she saw the courtyard of her house in Bethany. Perhaps the image was fresh from last night's dreams of marriage, for it was in that house that Yeshua and she were finally united, in fulfillment of the Law.

Was that Martha's face, bobbing gently in and out among the wavelets? Oh Martha! How you chastised me for neglecting my household duties to sit by my Lord and Master! Please understand, I could do nothing else, for he was the most important thing in the world to me.

"If I have not done enough, I beg your forgiveness once again," she told the face in the water. "Dear Martha, you were heavily burdened and I thought only of myself. I am truly sorry. But in your generous manner you remained my friend, my supporter, in the sisterhood of the Way. And Lo! You grew into your courage here in Gaul!

"Now you are a hero. People sing your praises! They tell their children and grandchildren how you subdued the dreadful monster, the Tarasque—and simply by bravely holding up a cross before him! You will become a legend, receiving great honor.

My dear sister in Yeshua, I miss you. How I long to see you again!"

Leaning closer, she spoke with heightened fervor to the reflection. But there, looking boldly back at her, was not Martha. Her own visage floated lazily among the ripples.

She saw herself for the first time as she really was—a thin, gaunt woman barely covered with tattered remains of a once beautiful robe. Her hair was matted, dirty, straggly. She recoiled, then peeked again at her face.

Her face! The face of the woman in the pool was— though soiled with neglect— smiling and happy. But the rest of her....

This will not do! she shouted aloud at the reflection, throwing a pebble to break it into a thousand ripples. On impulse, she stripped off her rags and, teeth chattering from the cold, plunged into the icy water.

"Aiee!" she screeched. But, resolute, she washed her body and her hair thoroughly clean before scrambling back out of the frigid bath.

Wet, cold and naked, the woman snatched up the full water jar and ran breathlessly back to her hermitage.

There, warmed by such exertion, she covered her nakedness with colorful cloth from the bundles of food, winding a piece of rope around her waist to hold the folds in place. With strands from the rope, she bound back her hair.

Now, she thought, running her hands in satisfaction over her newly tidy hair, Now I am ready for company!

* * * * *

On the drive home from Notre Dame du Cros, Karol took the wheel, while I kept my promise to tell her about dynastic marriage at the time of Jesus.

"Drawing upon Essene literature," I began, "and the works of Josephus, the Jewish historian who wrote in the 1st century CE, researchers have produced accounts of marriage customs among the Essenes. Two such authors are Barbara Thiering, in *Jesus the Man,* and Laurence Gardner in *Bloodline of the Holy Grail.*

"According to researchers, the Essenes were celibate, with propagation of the kingly lines of David and Zadok the exceptions."

"If they were celibate," asked Karol, proceeding down an avenue of trees joined at their tops in graceful Gothic arches, "how did they keep their numbers up?

"...Don't you love these trees?" she added, "I want a picture of them."

"I'll take one for you, next time we see them in time to snap it," I pledged.

"But to answer your question, they adopted. In those days, the way many people dealt with unwanted pregnancies was to leave children out in the desert to die. The Essenes rescued abandoned children and raised them."

"How awful, leaving children to die!"

"Of course. But unfortunately, it was common. Many cultures practiced infanticide, especially on baby girls. It still happens today, which is amazing when you realize birth control is available to nearly everyone."

"True," agreed Karol, honking politely at a tractor with attached disc harrow blocking most of the road. The farmer waved cheerily as she maneuvered past. I opened the passenger side window and waved back. He waved again, flashing a toothless grin. I think we both enjoyed the moment.

I closed the window. "Now, where was I?"

"Talking about the dynasties of David and Zadok. I presume they were the only exceptions to the rule."

"Yes. It was important that those bloodlines be kept going, so they developed a protocol for providing heirs. A very strict protocol."

"Which was?"

"First there was a betrothal. This would last for several years. No intimate relations were allowed. Then came the ceremony of the first marriage, held in September. This ceremony permitted sexual relations in the first half of December."

"Why December?...and *only* December?"

"Yes, only December, and only the first two weeks in December. This was so any resulting heir to the throne would be born during September, the holy month of Atonement. Remember, they were not only looking for a new king, they were also looking for a messiah, a holy savior."

Karol hugged the right side of the road while one more wild French driver, who had been bugging our tail, zoomed impatiently around us.

"Not going fast enough for him, I guess," she muttered *sotto voce.*

"They all drive like that," I agreed. "But when you put your lights on for safety, they very politely blink theirs back at you, thinking you left them on by accident. French drivers are polite, but impatient. Figure that.

"Can't."

"Anyway, as I was saying, after the first marriage ceremony they could have sex during the first two weeks in December. But if the woman didn't conceive, they had to wait until the next December to do it again."

"Bummer."

"Well, you or I might think so, but remember, they thought sex was sinful except for procreation. That's another concept that filtered down to today in organized religions."

"So what happened when the woman conceived?"

"If she didn't ever conceive, the man could divorce her. But if she did conceive, he could not.

"Her pregnancy would enable them to finalize the marriage, but only after the first three months. This was to guard against miscarriage during her first trimester spoiling the plan.

"Also, since the heir to the throne was expected to produce at least two sons, periods of celibacy were interspersed between periods of sexual activity, at carefully regulated intervals, and only in December."

"Ok, that all makes sense. But why is it, that Christian tradition holds Jesus was born of a virgin?"

191

"That's an easy one. Women were considered "virgins" until their second marriage. There was a mis-translation here. The original Hebrew word *almah* was taken to mean *virgin intacta*, when it really only meant woman who has not yet conceived a child. So a woman who is married can be called an *almah* until her final marriage. An *almah,* that is, 'virgin,' can conceive a child. After her final marriage, she was no longer considered an *almah.*"

"That certainly messes up the Christmas story."

"Yes, but does it matter to the basic Way that Jesus taught? *He* never claimed his mother was a virgin."

"True."

"But there was a different wrinkle in the story of his birthright. One of the problems about Jesus being the legal heir to the throne and messiah was that he was not born at the right time, according to the proper scenario."

"Does that mean what I think it means?" asked Karol, winking—or was it the sun shining into her eyes?

"Yup. It means Joseph and Mary let passion get the best of them before their first marriage and those permissible first two weeks in December. But their second son, James, was born in September like he was supposed to be. That's why there were two factions claiming the title, until James threw in his lot and supported his brother Jesus."

"Imagine that…as I recall, the New Testament does mention Jesus had brothers."

"Yes, it does," I confirmed.

"OK, Cinnie, now that I know all this, how does it fit in with Jesus and Saint Mary Magdalene?"

"Although references to their marriage were suppressed in the New Testament, there are clues," I responded.

"Anointing was an important part of dynastic marriage ceremonies. The first time Mary Magdalene anointed Jesus was when he was having dinner at the house of the Pharisees. (First marriage.) The second was at the home of Mary, Martha and

192

Lazarus in Bethany, just before Jesus made his dramatic entrance in Jerusalem. (Second marriage.) She used spikenard to anoint him, which is identified in the *Song of Solomon* as the symbol of marriage, and which, because it is so costly, can only be used by a messianic bride."

"So that's the second marriage? When Jesus went to Jerusalem, Mary was already pregnant?"

"That's the theory new research is turning up."

"Wow, that sure is a new twist on an old story, isn't it?"

"Yes, but once again, does it really make any difference to the real message Jesus gave us?"

"Not a bit," said Karol.

But after a moment's thought she asked, "There's something puzzling me. If Mary Magdalene was pregnant with their first child when Jesus was crucified, how could they have had two others after he died?"

"*Did* he die on the cross? Some researchers feel that's an open question too."

"Oh, I understand…."

We drove along the narrow roads in silence for a while, until we could see in the distance another of those beautiful avenues of golden, arched trees.

"This is your picture," I said, as we approached it. "Slow down."

Waiting carefully until there was no traffic behind us, Karol slowed the car, allowing me to photograph the gorgeous sight, (a symbol of France to both of us,) while hanging out the window like a madwoman, for a clear view.

Upon arriving back at LeThéron, we were invited by Philip and Margaret to join them and a group of their friends for dinner at a local restaurant.

It was Gypsy night. The *menu fixe* was Slavic food, and the accompanying music was provided by three Czechs— two sisters and a man, singing proper Slavic and gypsy songs. Much dancing and clapping and celebration—a perfect way to wrap up our week in Languedoc.

The next day we expected to drive about 6 hours along the Mediterranean coast (avoiding dreaded Béziers) to the Rhône River, then turn north along its East bank to Gordes, in the Lubéron Mountain area of Provence.

Along the way we were planning to meet Mary Magdalene's sister Martha, where she slew the monster, in the town of Tarascon.

Chapter Twenty

MARTHA

* * **

It was well that she was ready, for company was not long in coming. Not the crowd James, the Joseph, had promised to rally, but a single figure panting up the steep path barely a finger's length ahead of her donkey.

"Martha! Sister!" the woman cried joyously, embracing the exhausted visitor, assisting her into the cave's interior.

"A moment, dear sister, I must have a moment to catch my breath! Whatever possessed you to make such an inaccessible place your hermitage?"

"You know why, Martha, for I told you the last time you came to visit me, when you complained about the climb."

"Yes, yes." Impatiently, Martha removed the kerchief, from her gray hair, fanning her reddened face with it before tossing it carelessly aside. "Yes, you said you had enough of the material world and wished to spend the rest of your life in contemplation where nobody would bother you in seeking ecstasy."

"You remember well, but you have forgotten how to be our housekeeper," she chided gently, bending to pick up the cloth Martha had cast onto the floor. Folding it neatly, she placed the kerchief on a rock shelf.

"But I still love you greatly, sister, and welcome you to my abode. The climb becomes harder, the older the climber! For both of us now it is difficult indeed."

"Ah, yes," affirmed Martha. "Look at the two of us. Two old women with withered bodies, ready to bid goodbye to the world. And yet it seems..."

"...only yesterday?"

"Aye, it seems only yesterday that we welcomed the Master to our home in Bethany."

"It was more than thirty years ago, Martha. Just think what all has happened in that time! But wait a moment. Where are my manners? Please rest a moment on my bed over there, whilst I fetch you some refreshment, and tend to your beast of burden."

Martha settled gratefully among the furs, propping herself up on one elbow to watch her sister in the Way put a bowl of water on the ground before the donkey. He drank greedily. In an opened bundle she found a piece of bread and some honey, which she placed on the ground before Martha.

"Have you any wine?" Martha asked.

"You do not desire water?"

"I drank my fill at the spring in the forest. No, we should celebrate our reunion with wine."

"I'm sure Maximim brought some. Look at all the provisions he left!" Rummaging through an unopened package, she pulled out a canteen made from deer hide. "This must be wine. Here." She poured some liquid into the dipper, offering it to Martha. "We shall share it." Martha took a draught, passing the cup back to her sister, who also drank from the wooden vessel.

"So, why have you come alone to see me? Did not James intend to gather a group together?"

"Yes, and he is doing exactly that. But he dispatched me to make you ready." She appraised the figure clad in

196

clothing made from bundles and hair tied back with strands of rope.

" You do not appear as ragged as he described."

The woman laughed, quickly warmed and loosened by the sweet wine's heady elixir.

"Dear Martha, I saw myself in the pool of water by the spring, and the woman looking back at me, pleased me not. Therefore I have repaired my image."

"Soon you will be made as radiant as in your youth, for I have brought you beautiful raiment to wear, and ribbons to bind your hair."

"Ah," she sighed, "one cannot repair the damages of time, but I welcome the opportunity to try!" She giggled into the cup's ruby contents before sipping and passing it back.

"I feel younger already," Martha observed, pushing herself into a sitting position, head level with her sister on the floor. "Does this not remind you of days gone by?"

"Yes, but so much has occurred since then! My three children, my ministry, your ministry, your killing the monster— I have heard that story. Only this morning down by the pool I was thinking of you, and the legend that has grown up around your heroic act! Do tell me, were you terrified? Was the monster horrible?"

The woman sitting on the bed threw back her head in laughter.

"Oh, how the story grows!" she chortled gleefully. "It amuses me, so I have not refuted it, even if I could. But it was not at all what you have heard."

"No?"

"There never was a monster! It was only a small band of dark and dirty bandits. And I never slew a single person." She tossed her head disdainfully. A lock of hair loosened, falling across her brow.

"Bandits? Marauders?"

197

"Aye, a scraggly bunch, and I feared they would accost me and have their way with me, or worse." She pushed the lock back in place.

"Of course you were afraid. What did you do?"

"I scrambled up a rocky slope and climbed atop a huge boulder. The heathens were pursuing me at full run. I could almost feel their hot breath as they rushed to fall upon and ravish me."

"But what did you DO?"

"I called upon the mercy of the Mother and held out the cross I wore around my neck, thinking they might fear it had some power. I carried no other weapon."

"And that in itself subdued them? I can hardly believe this story."

"No," Martha remembered, suddenly serious, pushing away the nearly empty wine cup.

"No, a miracle happened. The Mother heard my cry and sent shafts of brilliant light from Heaven down through that cross, making it glow as if on fire."

"Ah! Mother of Mercy!"

"The heathens fell upon their knees at this terrifying sight and skulked away like whipped curs, tails between their legs, whimpering. They thought I was Holy Diana, about to hurl arrows of fire at them."

" Praise Mother!"

"Indeed." The women raised their hands, bowing their heads in gratitude.

"So, it must have been those vanquished bandits who started the tale of my supernatural powers. In the telling I grew into a saint, and the villains became transformed into that wicked monster, the Tarascon.

"In this way, such tales are embroidered from plain cloth! But in the end, the people only respected me more, and the Master's words through me." Martha smiled contentedly, hand upon her breast in a gesture of humility.

"As I," sighed the sister beside her. *"They have made golden tapestry fit for a king's throne out of some of my doings, before I retreated to this cavern—such as the story of how I was supposed to have kept a newborn baby alive for several years by suckling at its dead mother's breast."*

"Did you? I heard that rumor, but did not believe it."

"Of course not. It was an exaggeration. But that's not all. Later I was supposed to have restored her to life!

"What actually happened, I was attending the child's birth. The mother lost consciousness for several days, but regained it and returned to health. I held the babe to her breast so he would learn to suck while she was unconscious. But her body had not lost its functioning. It produced milk. The child survived, the mother did as well. But the people needed to believe I made a miracle."

"Perhaps the people are in need of miracles to support their faith."

"I suppose it is the nature of human beings."

"Perhaps so."

The donkey stood, eyes closed as if sleeping, while the sisters— bonded within the Way of the Master— sat together long, remembering. They recalled little stories of their life in the company of Yeshua, in the same manner as friends everywhere share the memories of good times, until the light faded into soft twilight.

At last, they kissed each other on both cheeks, looked lovingly into each other's eyes in the manner the Master had taught them, and retired into their separate world of dreams. One, to dream of days gone by; the other to dream of days to come.

Outside the cavern, a bird, fighting a losing battle with darkness, sang a plaintive song before settling into its nest.

Perhaps, like the auburn haired woman in the cave, it was longing for the return of its mate.

* * * * *

It was hard to say good-bye to Philip and Margaret, who had so quickly become our friends. As we finally drove away, little Iggy chased the car, barking furiously as if urging us to stay. At the end of the driveway he stopped, looking forlorn and more than a bit puzzled.

A final wave, and we were off towards Gordes.

We drove east in silence, except for navigational bulletins, until well past Béziers and safely onto the autoroute skirting the Mediterranean.

At that point it seemed the natural thing to plan the next part of our trip.

"What's left to find, Cinnie?" Karol asked, trying to fold the impossibly huge and unimaginably detailed Michelin map into manageable size in her lap.

"Hey! Watch that thing," I bleated, as part of it flapped between my steering wheel and the windshield.

"Sorry," she apologized, snatching it away and crumpling it into a plump, crackling mass. "There's just no way to control this monstrosity."

Opened to its fullest, the map would have filled the entire front seat of our little car, and part of the back as well. And that was only one little section of France! But I have to hand it to Michelin— nobody else can put so much information on a map.

"We still have to find Martha's remains in Tarascon, and Mary Magdalene's skull in St.Maximim-la-Sainte-Baume. And I hope we can find and climb to the cave where Mary was supposed to have spent the last 30 years of her life, naked except for her long hair and carried up to heaven seven times a day by angels."

"Yeah, sure."

"Well, that's legend. But in every legend there is a tiny grain of truth."

Karol finally had subdued Michelin into the square we were traveling. "I know that," she agreed.

"We have to turn south on D-15 off of D-999 to get to Tarascon."

"OK. Just let me know when we're getting close. Want to change drivers at the next rest area?"

"Sure. Did you forget about tomorrow?"

"Tomorrow?"

"Yes, the Ceremonial Procession in Les-Saintes-Maries-de-la-Mer. The day the Saints in the little boat get to go down to the sea."

"Good grief. Tomorrow is October 18th already. No, I didn't forget, I just lost track of what day it is."

"If we want to get there by 11, we'll have to leave Gordes very early. It's a long drive."

"Right. Two long drives in a row. Gas is so expensive, it's a good thing this little car gets good mileage."

The miles flew by, punctuated by changes of drivers at rest stops. We engaged in desultory conversation, everything from events of the past week to family relationships to memories of old college days, until we approached the tangle of roads around the city of Nîmes.

At that point Divine Guidance, instead of Michelin, must have taken over. *Somehow* we managed to end up in Beaucaire having lunch just across the Rhône from Tarascon.

Refreshed, we circled our way across the river and back (several times) to finally end up *somehow* in the parking lot of Tarascon's unique Collegiate Church of St. Martha.

We never did find out exactly what a collegiate church is, other than being a step higher than other churches, on the level of Nôtre Dame in Paris. Apparently Louis XI was very fond of either that church, or St. Martha, elevating it to that stature in the 15th century. And it was he who presented the church with a breathtaking reliquary of St. Martha, a copy of which resides in the little chapel of her name near the door.

It was the first thing we saw upon entering the portal. From behind a metal screen similar to those pulled across the doors and windows of jewelry shops in inner cities, peered the blue-green eyes of a dazzlingly beautiful woman. Her head and shoulders were draped in gold, her head surmounted with a jeweled crown, but the visage was lifelike in its coloring. So lifelike, that it seemed as if we were looking the real *Sainte Marthe* in the face. Her eyes seemed to stare right through us while we stood, paralyzed by the mesmerizing scene.

The bust of St. Martha is set upon a golden coffer adorned with arched panels showing, in blue and white porcelain, scenes from her life. But the center panel is different. In its niche rests one of her relics, something red, ruby red, *glowing* red.

In front of this relic's window kneels a tiny golden crowned figure, perhaps Louis XI himself, hands clasped in prayer and adoration. The whole reliquary is supported on the backs of four golden lions.

And, resplendent in its gold, rubies, emeralds and enamels, the figure just rests in glory and dignity, staring out at the world through those bright, turquoise eyes.

"So real!" Karol breathed in my ear. "It reminds me of those eerily lifelike figures in wax museums. You have the same feeling they might start to walk out of their display."

"This one can almost talk," I agreed.

"If she could, I wonder what she might say!" Karol was placing the lens of her camera into a hole between bars of the metal screen.

Good idea. I did the same. I forgot what we were talking about, trying to achieve that perfect picture.

Photography accomplished, we turned our attention to the church itself, which was large and beautifully decorated, although it evidenced a mixture of styles, due to restorations and additions. I took a picture of the ubiquitous Templar Cross upon a supporting column near the Baroque altar placed before Gothic arches. Somehow the mixture works.

A brochure in curiously written English allowed that the first chapel on that site was founded in AD 50. Just after Martha dispatched the Tarascon. One of the paintings was a gory rendition of the Saint, holding a cross above the writhing, fanged monster freshly feeding on the bodies of its victims.

Entering the crypt, however, was entering another world—one of silence, mystery and simplicity. Except for a bizarre grace note—the Saint's sculpted marble sarcophagus had holes in the sides, so adoring people could touch the body within.

"A little much," I muttered, as we ascended the stairs, and giving the beautiful reliquary a small salute, left by way of the front door.

"Yuk," confirmed my friend.

Finding our way back to D-99 we continued on the last leg of our long journey from Siran to Gordes, through St. Rémy and across the Durance River at Cavaillon.

Now we were in territory I remembered from the summer before!

So it was with the joy of recognition that I guided Karol along the D-2, northeast past the whale-like bulk of the Lubéron Mountain to the hilltop town of Gordes. Upwards we drove, steeply, past the Lavender Museum, the Stained Glass Museum, the village of stone huts called *bories,* to the circle by Gordes' main plaza.

Around the circle, further up the hill, just past the town limits, we turned into the driveway of *LaBorie*, the Bed and Breakfast I had stayed in last summer.

For another week, this was to be our new home.

TARASCON: Collegiate Church of St. Martha, St. Martha's Reliquary

Chapter Twenty-One

THE PILGRIMAGE

* * * * *

"Do you remember," Martha asked her sister the next morning, "the events of the first few weeks after being cast ashore in this new land?"

"Oh, many things happened," she answered, opening a bundle of food. "I remember most of them."

"Let me do that." Martha took the food from her hands, laying it out for them to eat. "Don't you recall, that's my duty?" She laughed lightly, dark eyes sparkling below the once-raven hair.

"Aye, your task among many others. But what in particular, pray tell, do you seek to consider from those early days?" She spoke through a mouthful of bread and cheese, "Ah, how much I now enjoy the taste of food!"

"I was thinking of the dedication of the little chapel we built, you and I, sisters Helena and Jacoba, and brothers Maximim, Sidonius and Simon Magus. Oh! I forgot. We were already calling Simon 'Lazarus' by then."

"While you're forgetting, don't leave out Sara."

"Aye, she was there too. It was only afterwards that Sara went off to minister to those dark people from the region of the Indus River."

The two women ate silently for a moment, each recalling her version of the dedication ceremony.

"It was on the first full moon of Autumn, was it not?"

Martha nodded enthusiastically, gesturing with a fresh date as if to illustrate her words.

"Yes, yes, so it was—and early in the morning before the globe of Artemis had been overshadowed by the dawn." She took a bite of the sweet fruit.

"Ah, what a dawn! Full of silvery magic. Moonlight in the clouds, moonlight on the water...."

"...and all of us were gathered in front of the little chapel, waiting for sunrise..." The two women followed each other's thoughts to completion, as if singing the refrain of a well loved poem.

"and all the village folk were there as well, still curious about us and the strange stories we were telling concerning the Master...."

"Oh, aye, they were curious, and more curious yet when Lazarus brought out the cross he had carved, holding it high to be gilded by the rising sun's rays."

"They did not yet understand it represented the Master." The woman touched the golden ring upon her finger to her lips. Her friend took little notice, lit by the fire of remembrance.

"As priestess, you raised your hands in prayer, and everybody knelt down upon the sand."

"Yes. And then Jacoba brought out a flute she had whittled from a piece of reed, clever woman..."

"... and played some stirring music she composed..."

"...while we all walked slowly down to the sea, carrying the cross."

"It seemed Great Sol had transformed the cross into pure gold," mused Sister Martha. "It was glowing, beautiful beyond words."

"Indeed it was." The Lady paused, smiling to herself, enjoying the memory. "When we waded into the sea, and turned to face the crowd of villagers, do you recall what happened?"

"Of course! From that clear sky, a bolt of lightning arched across the heavens…"

"…and thunder echoed from horizon to horizon."

"I can still see the fear and amazement upon their faces, until you calmed them."

"I did, yes, I remember. I told them to have no fear, for it was just a sign from Heaven approving what we were doing. And then I explained to them that the sea is the source of all life…"

"…you sprinkled the cross with sea water…"

"Just so. I told the crowd by this act we were bringing new life to all who would accept the Master's words."

"Oh, sister, it was so impressive! You looked like a goddess, standing there with the sunrise turning your hair to copper, even in your robe so tattered by the storm which wrecked our boat."

"I felt the power of the Word coursing through me. I felt Yeshua's presence behind me, urging me to speak."

"And so you did, back at the chapel. The villagers followed us into the nave, where the cross was placed in honor upon the altar. It was then you began to teach and minister to them. They grew to love you so much."

The two women sat, lost in that past time.

The priestess sighed heavily, head bowed. At length she murmured "I was full of the power of Yeshua in those days gone by."

Looking up, her face brightened.

"But Martha! He is coming back to claim me as his bride again! I have seen him! I know it! He has been giving me renewed strength, to meet him in the fullness of my power, as a bride should come unto her bridegroom! And it will be very soon! Perhaps even today!"

The other woman looked at her with a mixture of disbelief, and hope. "Perhaps," she comforted. "We shall pray for it.

"But now," she added, rising and pulling the other to her feet, "now we have to get you ready for your visitors. Just wait until you see what I have brought you!"

* * * * *

"What's a *borie?*" asked Karol as we approached the gate of our B & B. "Just a stone hut?"

"Yes," I answered, "except that they have been built here since prehistoric times. They served as shelters for both humans and animals until quite recently."

Just then Emanuel came to the gate to help us with our baggage. Down the few steps, we were greeted by three King Charles spaniels, numerous cats, and Christine, waiting in the kitchen.

"Bienvenue!" "Welcome!" "So good to see you again!" We were received warmly, and Karol duly introduced to our hosts and all their pets.

Moving through the living room to our bedroom, Karol could see how the house had been built onto an existing borie, for its ancient wall formed one side of the kitchen and breakfast area. The home is charming, tastefully decorated by Christine, who has a furnishings boutique adjacent to the Town Square.

Hanging upon the walls, two larger than life wooden angels bless the dining room. A huge wooden lion crouches at the entrance of the kitchen, guarding the harmonious collection of dried lavender, flowers, baskets and textiles filling the spacious rooms with color and fragrance.

A sunken sunroom is separated by glass doors from gardens and a large swimming pool—which in turn overlooks the town of Gordes, the valley stretching away to the Lubéron Mountain, and beyond.

In the garden, at a table by the pool, Karol and I quickly settled down with a *pastis*, the anise-flavored herbal aperitif so typical of Provence, to plan the next day's excursion to Les-

Saintes-Maries-de-la-Mer. There, we were going to observe one of the two yearly processions of the Saints, from the church down to the sea.

"We'll have to leave early, like you said, Karol. It's going to be a very full day."

"Right. It should be easy to find our way, though. We've already been over part of the route."

Just then Emanuel came to ask us what time we wanted breakfast—tea or coffee? Fresh squeezed orange juice or grapefruit juice? I knew from last year's experience breakfast would be a delight to all the senses.

As evening's dark tide swelled up the valley towards LaBorie, we finished off the sandwiches we had bought at a rest stop en route, enjoyed relaxing baths in the elegant stone-hewn bathroom and settled down into the cozy twin beds in our cheerily decorated bedroom for the night.

During the night, I awoke to hear rain gently tapping on the roof and splashing onto the porch outside our room. *Drat!* I thought. *Hope it doesn't rain on the procession of the Saints Mary-of-the-Sea.*

Breakfast was, as I had promised Karol, a wonderful experience. Snuggling up to the old borie wall beside the kitchen, our table was covered in a bright *Provençal* print tablecloth, upon which rested colorful china. Our individual, personal butter dish filled with country butter, and a basket of crusty fresh bread Emmanuel had fetched from the bakery as well as flaky, rich croissants were waiting to be enjoyed.

Next to the basket, a tray with more than a dozen different jams and jellies, each lid covered with a different colored print cloth, tempted us to choose among such treats as fig conserve, rhubarb jelly, wild honey and every imaginable fruit and berry preserve. And on the other side, a huge bowl of fresh fruit completed the colorful "still life" any artist would love to paint.

Outside, it was a different story. We drove down the hill through rain and mist. By the time we entered the *Camargue*

209

region leading to Les-Saintes-Maries-de-la-Mer the dense fog reminded me of Nova Scotia's worst possible weather.

I said a mental prayer to Mary…and…lo and behold! When we arrived at "Les-Saintes" the sky had cleared and the sun was shining.

The town, only mildly crowded with tourists on our first visit, was now crammed with pilgrims, tourists and gypsies. Parking in our favorite spot down by the seaside *promenade*, we found our way back to the Church plaza.

What a scene! Men in black velvet coats, print shirts and broad brimmed hats, carrying staffs with little prongs and colorful flags on the end, sat upon the backs of snorting, flower-bedecked white horses. The horses stood patiently waiting for Mass inside the church to end. Newspeople and tourists alike were aiming video cameras and snapping photographs.

It clearly was an important event, for literally thousands of people were crammed into the plaza at the church's doorstep.

I peeked inside, through the crowd, to see pews filled with women in traditional *Arlesienne* dress, and men in those dark velvet jackets. Hanging from the burial niche high above the altar were heavy ropes festooned with flowers and ribbons, by means of which the painted metal coffins of Saint Mary Helena and Saint Mary Jacoba had been lowered to altar level in ceremonies the previous day. Behind the altar they now rested, bathed in sunlight streaming from the windows above.

Ducking back into the plaza to rejoin Karol, I waited with her for the interminable Service to end. Eventually, the strains of an old Provençal hymn floated out to us.

"Il conduisit votre barque
A travers vents et mareés
Jusque vers notre Camargue:
Enfin, vous voilà sauvées.

(He guided your boat
Across winds and tides

Until coming to our Camargue
Finally, you found yourselves saved.)

En ces jours de grande fête,
Ces gens, venus de partout
Vous apportent leures requêtes:
O Saintes, écoutez-nous!

(In these great feast days
These people, come from everywhere
Bringing you their requests:
O Saints, hear us!)

When the singing ended, the *guardiens* formed their horses into double lines heading away from the church door. The crowd hushed. Video cameras whirred, recording the emergence of beautifully dressed ladies, starched caps upon their upswept hairdos, dignified men, followed by the parish priest, the crucifer and a group of costumed musicians beating drums with one hand and playing fifes with the other.

After the musicians, a white robed priest came forth, bearing a silver reliquary in the shape of a forearm, containing the arm bone of one of the Marys. With this he blessed the crowd through which the procession filed.

An expectant hush fell over everyone. Following the arm, four burly men appeared through the church doors. They were robed in bright blue, bearing on their shoulders two poles. Upon the poles rested a wooden platform, and upon the platform reposed the little blue boat carrying Saints Mary Helena and Saint Mary Jacoba.

Bobbing under the gait of the bearers, the two ladies seemed to be nodding their heads as they moved out of the dim church into the bright plaza. Bedecked by bunches of flowers, and resplendent in pink, sequined robes sparkling in the sunlight, the saints moved serenely and majestically through the streets,

211

surrounded by mounted *guardiens* and pursued by a throng of a thousand worshipers chanting:

"Vive les Saintes!"

"Vive Sarah!"

As the procession poured through the town streets, I found myself trotting right smack behind the horses, jumping over what horses leave behind, hopping up and down the curbs, determined not to lose sight of the Saints. The last I saw of Karol, she was aiming her camera at the procession from the relative safety of a sea wall.

Over dunes and rivulets the Saints were carried, until they reached the edge of the sea. There, the *guardiens* formed a semi-circle, horses knee deep in the water, turning to face the crowd, while the bearers entered the water, carefully turned the Saints around, and faced us too.

When a woman of special status reached down and splashed a few drops of water on each of the statues, a roar went up from the crowd.

"Vive les Saintes!

Vive Sarah!"

We all knelt in homage and respect. Thousands of people.

I cannot adequately describe the upwelling of pure emotion and love that emanated from that crowd. It was palpable. It was overwhelming. Every person's face radiated with devotion, faith, reverence.

Surely this was the heart of Provence!

I knew at that moment it was no idle legend that Mary Magdalene and her friends had come to the shores of Gaul.

They live here still.

"Vive les Saintes!"

"Vive Sarah!"

212

Chapter Twenty-Two

RESTORATION OF THE HOLY FEMININE

* * * * *

Running to the donkey which was peacefully dozing outside the cave, sister Martha gave it a slap on the rump.

"Ho! Back home you go! Trot down to your stable! James is waiting for you. Hup now!" The animal cheerfully ambled down the path, remembering full well the route to his stable and eager to return to a full measure of grain.

Turning towards the other woman, she picked up a packet carefully tied with golden ribbons. Mischievously, she held it out, eyes dancing.

"Here is your finery, dear sister—hasten to open it!"

One by one, the golden knots untied. The woman laid the package softly on the ground, opening soft cloth folds to reveal a fine linen garment of pure white, golden embroidery at the hem, neck and sleeves.

"I can hardly speak," gasped the Lady. "Never have I seen such a beautiful garment!"

"It was stitched for you by the women of Maximim's church. Go ahead, put it on!"

"N-no, it is much too elegant."

"It is our wish for you to wear it. Too long have you made do with so very little."

She slipped the garment of colorful patches off her sister's body and placed the new one over her head.

"Much better." Martha was looking around for a belt. She picked up the ribbon that had secured the package. "This will suffice. Let me tie it around your waist."

The Lady complied.

"Ah, now you look like an angel!"

"An angel? Hah! Already they are spreading rumors about me that I am a sinful woman. Paul has spoken badly of me ever since I bested him in the Alyscamps."

"Aye, but we who live in Truth know better. Now, we must do something about your hair."

After quite a struggle, the once-flaming locks were subjugated into waves, held in place by more of the golden ribbon. Nicely arranged, the color seemed to regain its former auburn glory.

Martha stood back to admire the overall effect. "Ah, yes, you look beautiful, my dear. Now for the finishing touch."

Out of the same package she withdrew a cloak of midnight blue, spangled with silver stars and mystical symbols.

"The Lady gasped in delight. "How heavenly! Could I… Should I…?"

"Of course, my dear. Sara brought it from the dark ones of the East. It is to honor you as their queen."

"I am queen of no country," she stated flatly, shrugging her shoulders into the magnificent cloth, "but only Queen to Yeshua."

Yet, as if donning the cloak had triggered some latent power, she turned to a niche in the rock, withdrawing a covered basket. Placing it on the floor, she reverently extracted three items, the empty alabaster jar from Yeshua's anointing, a book, and a human skull. The jar, she held in one hand; the skull and book she laid at her feet.

From the same recess she picked up a staff of cedar.
Buds were bursting from each knothole.

Thumping it upon the floor, she turned to face the
opening of the cave, drawing herself to full height, announcing
to the world in general—
as regally as any monarch—
as beautiful as any queen—

"I have been saving these.
"Let them come, for now I am prepared."

* * * * *

I was still singing and shouting "Vive les Saintes! Vive Sarah!" along with the crowd. At this point we were following our beloved Saints back through the streets of Les-Saintes-Maries-de-la-Mer to the church, borne along by the pressing flow of pilgrims, worshipers and tourists.

Through the door filed the procession—I, carried along with the rest of the people. Standing by a stone column inside, I watched the two lovely ladies in their boat being returned to the niche in the wall. As solemnly as ever, the dark haired one held her free hand out in blessing, the other hand clutching the covered chalice I had once thought was the Holy Grail.

Now I knew it could be believed as that, but much, much more—a jar of fragrant ointment, a symbol of the Cosmos, the womb, cup of sustenance to feed people's spirit—on and on, many levels deep.

Symbols. Ceremonies are symbols with many depths of meaning… the statues, procession, cup, flowers, cross, priests, relics, the church itself—all symbols.

If you could comprehend the totality of these symbols, I thought, *you would understand everything there is to know.*

What do you suppose are the truths symbolically represented this day in Les-Saintes-Maries-de-la-Mer?

215

By now, I believed, I could answer my own question.

My answer is that nearly two millennia ago a group of people arrived in this place, fugitives from persecution of their new religion,

-that here they spread their belief in Love and Faith and Brotherhood,

-that here these immigrants remained, winning hearts and souls of the people,

-that here, though ignored by Scripture, they became a living part of the traditions and culture of this region, traditions we were witnessing this very day—

—and that their presence in this land affected the course of History!

At the precise moment of my great realization, the priest began a new ceremony. Enough already! I squeezed through the crowd, to find Karol waiting outside. She had discovered Ross, who had driven down from Castlefranc with one of the sisters who run it, for the occasion. They were having coffee on the terrace of a plaza restaurant.

With them, we enjoyed watching a group of young girls in traditional costume, dancing to the music of the fife and drum band, while we sipped cappuccino. Presently, the crowd dissipated, the church emptied, we said goodbye again to Ross, to reenter the now-empty house of worship.

Deserted, the interior felt even more sacred than when it had been filled with people. Behind the altar, a few individuals stood quietly touching the painted coffins of the Saints Mary, silently praying.

The coffins themselves, strapped together in a steel frame for raising and lowering to the altar, were painted with scenes illustrating their legend.

St. Mary Helena's coffin showed the two women in a wave-lashed boat, helpless, without oars, appearing very distressed. The black haired Saint Mary, dressed in red with a black cloak, is shading her eyes with one hand, looking for land.

216

The other Saint Mary, wearing red with a blue sash, touches hand to heart. Each of them is clutching the boat's railing for support in the turbulent storm.

St. Mary Jacoba's coffin depicted the boat, beached at last. The woman in black is walking, hands raised in thanksgiving, on the sand. The woman in red is placing one foot out of the boat, preparing to disembark. Above the horizon of a calm sea, the sun glows, perhaps having just risen to herald a new day.

Or perhaps a new era.

While Karol sat in prayerful meditation, I walked up to the iron coffins, touching them reverently. Who really lay within? According to tourist literature, the skeletons of two middle-aged women were found in 1448 under the crypt, and placed in coffins. These were burned in the Revolution, but some of the relics were rescued, later to be entombed inside the very coffins beneath my fingers.

Mystery, still mystery. Surely they must have been women held in high esteem, to have been buried in that place of honor beneath the crypt. But if faith can create truth, the two ladies whose remains rested within were definitely Saint Mary Jacoba, said to be the wife of Cleophas, brother of Jesus' father— and Saint Mary Helena, also known as Salome, consort of Simon Magus, who was later called Lazarus.

I rejoined Karol. Together we descended into the candlelit crypt to say goodbye to Sarah. The dark-skinned beauty stood as before, wrapped in her purple cape, but now fresh flowers were scattered at her feet and tucked into her robes.

She smiled, as always, while we talked to her, fondly stroking her robe.

"Your procession will come in seven months' time," I crooned. "Next May 24th, a Gypsy Queen will be crowned, and you will be carried to the sea, like your sisters were today. They will make that journey again, but not until the day after you. May is your special pilgrimage, not October. Be patient. May will soon be here."

217

Karol stared. "You sound like a mother hen clucking to her chicks," she said.

The statue just continued smiling enigmatically, surrounded by the floral offerings of her Gypsy children. More candles than usual were lit in that warm crypt.

Karol and I each added another, and left Sarah, regretfully, for the last time.

On the hour and a half drive back to Gordes, we spoke of the Gypsy mystery.

"The name comes from the word 'Egypt,'" Karol offered, looking up from a guidebook.

"Yes, I've read that too. But the Gypsies didn't originate in Egypt."

"Where, then?"

"I don't think anyone really knows. Some say they are Atlanteans, remnants of the legendary land that sank beneath the sea. Others say they came from India."

"That sounds like the best bet."

"Yes, but they sure traveled around a lot. Probably did move through Egypt, and most of Europe as well. Now they are everywhere."

Karol leaned back against the car's headrest, looking dreamily out the window. "There must be a lot of stories about Sarah. Like why do you suppose the Gypsies took her as their patron saint?"

"Don't know. She is supposed to have come over on that little boat with the Marys, Lazarus, Maximim and the others. She is portrayed as a black slave, from Egypt. There is a story that she was left behind, but begged to come too—so one of the Marys threw her cloak over the side and Sarah walked on it to the boat."

"Walked on water, eh? Pretty impressive."

"Then another is, she left this area and went to live with the Gypsies, ministering to them, doing miracles, as any Saint worth

218

her salt must do. Her skin was dark, like the Shulamite in the *Song of Songs*."

"And like the Egyptians, and the Gypsies."

"Right," I declared—"and like the Black Madonna."

"Of course, she *is* a Black Madonna!"

"The dark, mysterious aspect of Great Mother," I agreed. "But she isn't dark because of smoke in the crypt."

"I know that," Karol said, adding, "I guess this is the way people have explained away many of the Black Madonnas."

"The famous one in Poland—they say she was in a fire."

"Fire, schmire. People just don't want to see the truth." Karol closed the book with a snap. "I'll bet more and more information will come to light about the Black Madonnas."

"Sure. The same way there are so many appearances of the White Madonna these days—the Virgin Mary. Now there are more and more statues being discovered of her dark counterpart. It's part of what has been foretold."

"What do you mean, foretold?"

"It has been prophesied that at this time, when we are entering into the Age of Aquarius, the Holy Feminine will be restored to her rightful place in the Godhead. That's what *Revelations* is about."

"Not just war and disease and earth changes and famine?"

"No. It's about these times we live in. When we have polluted the earth. When greed and power— the Anti-Christ— rules the world."

"Isn't the Anti-Christ supposed to be a person?"

"Maybe, but to my way of thinking it is a symbol, a symbol of negative power, lust and greed. I believe all of *Revelations* is symbolic."

"What about Armageddon, the final war between Good and Evil?"

"How can there be a war between them if they are only different aspects of the same thing? No, Armageddon is really

219

about what it takes for us to wake up, to cleanse the hearts of men, and the earth which sustains us."

"Then what is the Restoration of the Holy Feminine?" Karol asked. "What does it really mean?"

"It means balance, equality of all things male and female, yin and yang, in dynamic but equal relationship."

"Well, when is that supposed to happen?"

"After the cleansing, after the healing, then comes the Restoration of the Holy Feminine."

"The Golden age, the thousand years of peace?"

"I hope so."

"But what about the Second Coming of Jesus?" Karol pursued with interest.

"It is here," I declared. I believe it has always been here, in those who live with Love in their hearts."

"Yes," she sighed, "seems like everything is metaphor."

"Many, many layers," I agreed.

"But what of this 'Restoration of the Holy Feminine?' When will we start to see it happening? Soon?"

"Not *soon*," I stated flatly, as we started chugging up the hill to Gordes, "but *now*.

"The time is now."

Chapter Twenty-Three

CAVE OF THE MAGDALENE

* * * * *

Come, they did, in twos and threes, struggling up through the forest.

First, dear James appeared, in the company of Maximim and Lazarus. Entering the cavern, the three men fell to their knees in astonishment and adoration, at the woman's transformation from tattered Crone to regal Goddess.

"Lady!" they cried in unison, "Our Lady!"

"Your friend," she replied, indicating they should rise. "Always your friend, and your sister." She kissed each of them in turn, on both cheeks, as was the custom.

"I hear the sounds of others ascending the path behind you. Pray, will you help sister Martha prepare the feast, while I bid them welcome?"

"As you wish." There was no mistaking their deference. The four busied themselves dragging bundles of food out onto the cave's wide ledge at the top of the trail, spreading each cloth on the ground beneath its bounteous contents. Dried fish, loaves of bread, honey, figs, cheese, fruits, nuts, water, wine—a feast fit for kings and queens!

"Tamar! Justus! Josephes!" She ran to embrace her children, as they and their spouses, shepherding a small flock of children, emerged from the woods. "I am overcome with joy to see you and the little ones!" Much like a piece of

221

honeycomb surrounded by buzzing flies, the little children clinging to her skirt, the group happily stumbled up the rest of the rocky path, rejoicing in each other's company.

Following her tribe came friends and villagers, until the ledge was crowded with visitors, eating and drinking, laughing, singing, children playing...

And through the celebrating crowd she passed, greeting each guest personally, inquiring about their health, their lives, their loved ones... the perfect hostess, the much beloved queen of hearts...long into the late afternoon.

The valley below rang with sounds of joy, wafting down across the treetops.

Yes, they loved her, in this land.

At last, sated, the guests sat quietly, while a young goatherd played songs of love and longing upon his flute.

As the last plaintive sounds departed on the breeze, the woman in white wrapped the cloak of stars around her shoulders, placed the skull and book upon her meditation rock, and grasped the alabaster jar in one hand. With the aid of the cedar staff, she climbed nimbly up, to stand beside the skull.

"My dearest friends." She spoke softly, her words directed to the silent crowd at her feet.

"My dearest friends." She began again, louder this time, for trees and rocks and all Creation to also hear.

"Thank you for coming to be with me this special day.

"Long have I separated myself from you, lost in my silence, lost in my longing for the Master, my true Love, my cherished Husband.

"Long have I sought the strength to go forth into his world above. In trying to approach his world, I have neglected my own. I suffered. I fasted. I retreated from your support and good company.

"But that is over now. As you see, I have regained much of my former strength. "Today is to be, once again, my

wedding day." She held up her hand with the golden ring upon her finger, for all to see. "Yes, once again, my wedding day!

"For Yeshua has appeared to me! He has come down from Heaven to teach me!"

A murmur of surprise rippled through the crowd around her feet.

"Aye, verily, he has appeared to me, and has shown me many wonders. And he has given me this ring in token of our coming reunion. He will come again soon to take me to his kingdom—he has promised! And I am ready!"

She lowered her hand to her heart. "But before I go, there are things I must relate to you. He has taught me about the future. He has shown me torture and healing, war and peace, darkness and enlightenment. He has given me a mission down through the ages to come."

The crowd stirred in wonder and growing excitement, responding to her own.

"He has given me strength and understanding, the gifts of power and self knowledge." Her face became more animated with every word, the people more aroused in their agitation and curiosity.

"He has given me knowledge of the past and of the future!"

"Say then, what it is!" cried out one of the men.

"Aye, tell us!" echoed another.

"I share his vision for the world! He has told me! He has shown me!"

"Tell us! Tell us!" the people pleaded.

"I see the future of mankind!" She was shouting now, drawn up to her full height, grasping the cedar staff tightly. Her face seemed to glow with some sort of inner illumination.

"People! Friends! Know that fate is in your own hands! You must not fall away! You must follow what he taught us!"

"Yes, yes!" The voices of the crowd found rhythm, pulsing like a heartbeat.

"He has given me the gift of Prophecy!"

The litany rose in volume and fervor. *"Tell us! Tell us! Tell us!"*

And now it became a chant—

"Prophesy, Our Lady! Prophesy to us!

"Tell us, Our Lady!

"Prophesy!"

"Prophesy, our Lady! Prophesy to us!

"Tell us, Our Lady!

PROPHESY!"

* * * * *

After our customary little bedtop dinner picnic at LaBorie, it was difficult to fall asleep. Not because of the odd assortment of nuts, olives, yogurt, cheese and bread comprising our repast, but because of the memory of so much color, pomp, fervor, excitement, in the pilgrimage of the two Saints Mary to the sea!

The images behind closed eyelids would not fade into dreams, but repeated themselves, over and over, like a stuck film. Horses, pink sequined statues, bobbing lifelike on the shoulders of the faithful, music, crowds babbling excitedly in many languages, dancing, colorful costumes, flags flapping gaily in the breeze, sun, water, passion, adoration, tradition….

"Vive les Saintes!

Vive Sarah!"

At long last, the fervent chanting blended into the real sound of rain falling on the roof, carrying me off to sleep in my snug little boat of a bed.

Morning presented itself as cold and misty as the day before. And, in the same manner as the day before, as soon as we descended from Gordes into the valley below, it cleared into bright, brisk Autumn.

Fortified by another of Christine and Emanuel's fabulous breakfasts, we were off to try to find the Magdalene's cave. A friend, Kenna, had provided us with directions, but warned us the cave had been isolated by a rockslide when she had tried to reach it in the spring. We were hoping the slide had been cleared by the time of our arrival and the cave reopened.

It is a much-repeated legend that Mary Magdalene had spent the last years of her life there as a hermit, so often repeated that it is accepted as truth by most of the population. But it is also known to have been a place of pilgrimage by Pagans long before Mary's time.

Once more, a sacred place for millennia past has metamorphosed into a shrine for the present. That spiral again! Earth energies were there from the beginning. People simply recognize the sanctity of the spot, continuing to build the sacred edifices of their cultures upon it, one upon another.

Like the Cathedral at Chartres. It rises over underground watercourses. And the Abbey at Glastonbury. Even the little church we visited at Vals. All the great cathedrals were built on places known to be sacred from antiquity, usually connected with springs or wells—life-giving water.

The same thing happens to religious holidays. Jesus' birth was moved to compete with Pagan Winter Solstice. Easter and Passover both coincide with the cycles of the full moon and Spring Equinox. Even Beltane became May Day, celebrated on one hand by veneration of the Virgin Mary, and on the other hand by parades of tanks and guns through Moscow's Red Square.

Go figure.

Sorry, I'm off on an aside again.

Karol and I found the tiny town of Nans-les-Pins, near the foot of the high Massif de la Sainte Baume, but not before winding our way through many detours—

    —up and down winding little roads,

    —through winding little towns,

    —in winding little valleys,

225

—by winding little streams.

Most definitely not a boring drive!

After what seemed like a very long time, we nosed the Renault up to a fence in the parking lot of what appeared to be some sort of forest preserve.

Darn! There was a sign in big red letters:

"DANGER!
Chutes de pierres.
Accès a la Grotte Interdit.

You didn't have to speak French to get the drift. The Cave was still closed by a dangerous rock fall.

"D'ya think it's still really closed? It was early spring when Kenna was here—over seven months ago." To my way of thinking, it seemed more than enough time to clear a rock fall.

"Right, Cinnie. Maybe the French work slowly. But then again…."

"Good thought, Karol." (We know each other so well we often don't have to finish sentences.) "Maybe it's just to keep too many nosy tourists away."

"Only one way to find out."

"You're right. Let's go."

Paying our respects to a long dead tree near the sign, for all the world looking like a hooded guardian of the forest about to pounce upon senior citizens who disobey the law, we hoisted up our backpacks and started up the trail.

Immediately, we were in deep, primeval, forest. The path quickly steepened, over fallen logs, mossy rocks and past shrines standing, shrouded by the trees, in stony silence.

It was more of a climb than we anticipated. Breathless, we paused from time to time to sit upon a stone or lean against a tree, listening to birds, watching butterflies, observing leaves falling in gold and russet glimmers from the forest canopy.

The higher we climbed, the more mysterious and magica

226

I became the forest. Moisture began filtering through the treetops, wrapping us in gentle mist. Sunshine, penetrating from time to time, cast beams of light down upon our heads like messages directly from God. Sounds from below faded away. The only things interrupting silence were our muffled footsteps and labored breathing.

But no! A new sound softly intruded, musical and gentle. It grew louder as we climbed, until rounding a bend we encountered pure water, dripping from a hidden spring into a basin some pilgrim had fashioned from stone and concrete.

Through the rock wall protruded a wooden spigot, gushing forth the coldest, cleanest, clearest, most welcome water we ever tasted.

"It can't be far to tree line now, " Karol panted, stepping more quickly towards refreshment. "Perhaps this was the water source for the Magdalene's cave."

It surely could have been.

In gratitude, we slaked our thirst, washing the hike's sweat off our faces, resting on the basin wall.

"I think I'll take a couple pictures here," I said to Karol, perched upon the wall. "The forest is so lovely in this mist."

I was not disappointed. Later, one of the photographs clearly showed an angel's light, brightly shining through the trees.

We climbed a bit further, expecting the forest to end around every curve of the path. At last it did.

Emerging into sunlight at the base of a rocky cliff, we discovered concrete stairs ascending out of sight behind a wide ledge—and a chain across the stairs with another sign forbidding entry, in the strongest possible language!

"Oh well, " I sighed in disappointment. "Maybe I should remember it's not arriving at the destination that's important, but the journey."

"Yes," echoed Karol. "Perhaps it was the climb through the magic forest itself that was the highlight of this day."

I thought she was right.

227

That is, I thought she was right until later in the afternoon, when we found ourselves face to face with Mary Magdalene.

NAS-LES-PINS:
Mountain of Mary Magadalene's Cave

Chapter Twenty-Four

MEETING MARY

* * * * *

Coming down from the mountain was a lot easier than going up. And quicker. But the quiet softness of that primeval forest lingered in our spirits all the way back to the town of Saint-Maximin-la-Sainte-Baume, whose Basilica is said to guard the skull of Mary Magdalene.

The town itself was far from bustling, but we found a *brasserie* that served salads and such, on the Town Square. There we pacified the enormous appetites created by our climb up "Mary Mountain."

"Sure do wish we'd been able to get into the cave," mumbled Karol, diving into her *Salade Niçoise* (tuna, potatoes and black olives) with relish. I mean she was diving into it with relish, not that relish was served…well, *you* know….

"Next time," I promised, scarfing down my own with the help of that ubiquitous and wonderful French bread. You dip it in the dressing, see….

"There's always something left for next time. Remember, we said that about Greece? When we couldn't get to Delos?"

"Yes, and we still haven't. But I think this will be different. For some reason, it seems like home here."

"Feel it in your bones?" That's what they say. And speaking of which, let's go to the Basilica to look at some of Mary's. That's really what we're here for, isn't it?" I asked rhetorically, feeling a little chirpy from the calories.

229

"Yeah, that's the big event. But there's still a lot to see around Provence—little hilltop towns, castles, the Matisse Chapel in Vence…."

"We'll do those too," I promised Karol. "Regular tourists."

"It's a deal."

So we paid the *addition* and walked down a cobbled street towards the Basilica. With buildings on both sides marching almost up to the front door, there's no way to take a photograph of the entire edifice. So I settled for a view of the center façade, a square tower whose simple archway was decorated by a red and yellow, *fleur-de-lis* embellished, striped banner hanging above a wooden door.

The carvings over the door caught my attention. On the left, St. Maximim clutched an open book in his curiously lotus-like right hand. On his left side, a double lily sprang full bloom from some sort of spiral base—and could that be a lamb and a staff beside it? Hard to tell—the doors had suffered some damage.

The other panel showed Mary Magdalene, hands clasped in prayer, surrounded by all her icons and her flowing hair. It was easy to spot them now—the fruitful tree, crucifix, open book, alabaster jar, and skull. Both figures rose, waist high, from the cup of a classical acanthus leaf.

It is said St. Maximim and Mary Magdalene were good friends—that he buried her when she died, right here at this place. Of course there was no church at the time—or was there? It seems, as previously noted, all the churches built in the 10th to 13th century were placed over earlier structures.

But the story goes, it is in this sacred edifice that her remains remain… and we wanted to see them.

Entering the Basilica led us into a space of sharp contrast to the plain, unprepossessing exterior. It is the finest example of Gothic architecture in Provence. Though dim, and somewhat neglected, the interior with its high vaulted windows, beautiful statues and ornate altar seemed graceful and elegant, pleasing to the eye.

Above the altar hung a golden sunburst of rays, figures and angels surrounding a stained glass panel depicting the Holy Spirit in the form of a dove.

Incredibly beautiful.

Another picture of loveliness was the golden clad statue of the Virgin Mary standing, arms outstretched in blessing, upon a blue globe encircled by a snake.

But most beautiful of all was another statue, elevated in a prominent place of honor. Before a light blue, star-studded background stood a white marble Madonna and child. The child is holding a golden cross upon an orb; the mother, a golden scepter. With a little imagination, one can make out shadowy forms of people behind them.

She stands, holding her child, upon a pedestal adorned with two winged griffins, embracing a shield surprisingly bearing a *Cathar Cross!*

And above her head unfurls a ribbon upon which are written the words: "*JE SUIS LA MERE DE LA SAINTE ESPÉRANCE*"

—"I am the Mother of the Holy Hope."

In humility of heart I know that she is right, though I may be perceiving that statement in my own personal way.

But some people must not feel as entranced with The Magdalene. On a wall, a larger than life sized painting depicts Mary Magdalene, holding skull and jar, walking beside a budding branch and looking up to angels in Heaven. It has been rent from breast to toe by the angry sword of some unknown fanatic.

Karol and I walked down into the crypt. At a turn in the staircase, a niche holds a life sized statue of Mary Magdalene, nose tainted with the smoke of votive candles—or the hands of the faithful reaching across an iron railing to touch her?

She is reclining, hands clasped in prayer, against a rock, jar and cross at her side.

"Karol, do you notice anything odd about the way her hands are clasped?"

231

"Well yes, the thumb and first finger of her left hand cross under the thumb of her right hand," said Karol, trying to do it with her own fingers. "Not natural."

"Right, you'd have to do it on purpose. Remember the other time we saw her hands clasped oddly? On the altar painting in the church at Rennes-le-Château. The one that Béranger finished painting himself."

"Mean anything?"

"Don't know, but secret societies and street gangs have special hand signs."

"You're jumping to conclusions, Cinnie."

"Maybe, but I love mystery."

Such casual conversation stopped abruptly, when we turned the corner of the stairs. There, at the end of a sarcophagus-lined vault, presiding in golden glory, was the smiling skull believed to be of Mary Magdalene herself.

All that separated us from her was an iron railing and shield of Plexiglas. Stunned by the sharp reality of encounter, we gawked rather impolitely at the Lady. Inside a coiffure of gold, head and shoulders supported by two golden angels, the skull gazed serenely back. But it seemed to be more than just a skull.

Her sightless eyes seemed to be all-seeing, all-knowing, boring into our very souls and hearts.

The moment suddenly felt totally sacred. We closed our mouths and clasped our hands quite unintentionally in a natural gesture of prayer.

Imagine! Here we were, face to face with Mary Magdalene!

Well, Mary, I thought, *we've come at last. All this time we have been searching, finding traces of you everywhere, and finally we have found you.*

Whatever adventures we had experienced, whatever mysteries we had uncovered all dissolved into that holy instant. Time stretched into everywhere, and nowhere.

In that minute lived past and present, legend and history.

That encounter was too sacred to put into words—

For that moment encompassed the whole of our experience.

There was nothing more to think or say—

Only to feel.

Days later, on our way back to the Marseilles airport under starry skies long before dawn, Karol and I talked over the adventures of our journey.

After the Basilica of St.-Maximim-la-Ste.-Baume, we had visited nearly every village in the Lubéron. We had explored Abbeys, museums, historic places, castles, good food, good wine, good company—filling the remaining few days with pleasure of all the senses.

But we agreed those moments in the crypt with Mary Magdalene were the most precious of all. Those moments were the point of it all, the pivot point of knowing.

Knowing what?

—That I believe she did come here; the legends contain this truth.

—That, never a sinner, she changed the course of history and the Roman church.

—That whatever her relationship with Jesus, she represents the emerging hidden aspect of the powerful feminine spirit.

—That one day soon the Holy Feminine will be restored in balance with the Holy Masculine, and the world will be better for it.

—That the most important journey is the one which leads to understanding,

—and that we have started down that road to knowledge.

* * * * *

233

"St. MAXIMIM-LA-SAINTE-BAUME:
Reliquary Containing the Skull of
Mary Magdalene"

Chapter Twenty-Five

ASCENSION

* * * * *

With a wave of her staff, she silenced the crowd. They looked up at her, faces animated by expectation.

Listening…waiting….

She breathed deeply, stretching her awareness past the people, past the cave, past the sky. Those nearest could see some sort of connection, for as she turned her eyes towards Heaven, a pale shaft of light seemed to reach down to encompass her figure, bringing glints of gold to her hair and eyes, coloring the white of her gown.

"My children," she began, voice trembling with emotion. Then something altered. It was as if the Holy Spirit had entered by fire, transforming humility and reticence into strength and wisdom.

"Children of Heaven, hear me! The Master bids me speak to you!"

…Murmurs of wonder from the group at her feet….

"Speak, then, Mother!" implored Tamar rising on her knees to touch the blue cloak's hem.

Her mother bent down to kiss her brow.

"This, you all know, is my beloved daughter, Tamar. I too have a mother, long departed from this life. And she had a mother— and her mother, a mother —and so on to the first woman created out of God.

"Tamar has daughters, and they will have daughters; their daughters will also have daughters, and so on until the end of the world.

"They will carry the spirit of God to the ends of the earth, through all time. They will work with the sons of man, in perfect harmony, to manifest God's Heaven upon mother earth—for Heaven and Earth are destined to be One!"

An old woman sitting near the edge of the cliff spoke up, her thin voice crackling with age. "As above, so below— that's what the Master taught us."

"Aye, sister, so it is, though imperfectly. So it will be, sometime long hence."

"What of men?" asked her husband, lovingly stroking the old woman's hand. "What will they carry into the future?"

"Dear brother, it will be men who carry the energy to build, to invent, to do great things. It will be men who labor and provide, and women will create. You know the Master always told us all people carry the spirit of God."

A shadow passed overhead, darkening the cliffside, mirroring the depths to which her awareness began to descend. Her body shifted subtly. Tears gathered, ready to fall.

"But my children," she continued, in a lower tone, " I have been shown much sadness, in visions of the future.

"Woe unto women! for the Sacred Feminine shall be hidden like the pomegranate seed within its fruit—carrying the spark of life until the time is right. Only then will the fruit ripen, falling open to spill its healing seeds upon the earth.

"You, women, shall be those seeds, bringing forth much needed healing—since great misfortune awaits the daughters of men, and the earth!"

She paused, watching her words flow out over the people who came to honor her, words carrying the darkness of a widow's veil.

After long moments of heavy silence, she lifted her face to the sky, shaking her staff in anger.

"Mourn, women! Let flow your tears— for you shall bring forth your daughters into a world of terror!" Her voice rose in strength with every breath, her face distorted with rage at what she suddenly could see. She cried aloud, ablaze with the same intense prescience as prophets of old...

"I see visions of torture, pillage and rape! I see women thrown into the fire because of the jealousy of men...

"...babes put to the sword within their mothers' wombs!

"I see the mutilation of children as they enter womanhood, burning of brides, female priests and healers being stoned...crones neglected...newborns girls left to die....

"AIEEE!" She sobbed, leaning heavily upon the staff, overcome with grief. Keening, moaning, the people listening began to weep as well.

All at once she drew herself full upright, voice resounding with passion.

"Mourn, too, for the earth!— for mankind will despoil her bounty with neglect and poison!" she cried.

"Mourn, too, for the sky!— for mankind will pour venom into the air we breathe!

"Mourn, too, for the seas!— too full of bitterness for fish to live!

"Mourn, too, for animals, friends and servants of humans!— for they will be abused and neglected.

"But mourn most deeply for the fate of mankind, because human beings will come to the very edge of destroying their own existence!"

The crowd sat nearly paralyzed with sorrow and fear.

"Mother!" pleaded Tamar, "Is there no hope? No hope at all?"

With great force of will, the woman pulled herself back from that abyss she had entered, the black casket of pain she had opened. Extending her arms, tears still glistening through her eyelashes, she smiled the warm smile of a mother.

237

"Yes, my children, there is hope. As long as there is humankind, there is hope.

The feminine spirit is the Hope, which will finally emerge, bringing the earth back into harmony.

"At the very worst time of chaos, when people think that God has deserted them, seeds from the pomegranate will scatter across the earth, healing and restoring."

She paused for a moment, letting the metaphor sink deeply in.

"Listen carefully, my children. Very soon I shall leave you. I go to rejoin Yeshua in the world above. But I shall not desert you. He will always be your father, and I, your mother.

"No, mother, do not leave us!" Tamar rose to her knees, begging. The woman hardly noticed.

"I give to all of you this legacy— the knowledge that the Sacred Feminine, unified, is the Hope of mankind, and that it is carried in every man and every woman, waiting for the right time to burst forth.

"And I shall not desert you, my children! Never!

"In all that may come to be, I will be there, just beyond the veil. And I shall part the veil when mankind is most in need of hope and reassurance.

"I shall appear to you, in places flung far around the world! I shall appear in the blue robes of the Holy Virgin, and in the dark robes of the Black Madonna, for I am the hidden aspect of the Mother of God. We are one and the same.

"I shall appear to children, who have open hearts ready to receive me, and I shall appear to old people who believe in me through the wisdom of their faith.

"I shall honor a humble farmer in a land far away, placing my image upon his cloak to bear witness of my existence. And I will be the hope of his ancestors.

"I shall dance upon the towers of churches, cause the sun to spin in the Heavens, come to the aid of soldiers in battle. I shall drop petals of flowers from above. My presence

will be sensed in fragrance of the rose. I shall cause my images to shed tears for the fate of mankind and womankind.

"I shall appear at springs, and on mountaintops. I will come in bright light, down from the heavens to heal and succour. I shall work miracles for those who have faith in me.

"Whenever you see my image in any of my manifestations, be aware I am there for you.

"Whenever you look upon the symbols I carry, be reminded of my strength, my power and my love.

"This staff will support your faith and hope!

"This jar will be the cauldron containing all possibilities, the holy cup of understanding!

"This skull will represent the wisdom you carry, the spark of God within!

"And this book will represent the true words of the Master. It need not have many pages, for his truth distills into just two charges—Love God and love your brother, and everything is your brother."

Reassured—nay, filled with the joy of her promises, the people at her feet sat raptly listening to every word. Never to be deserted! Always to have hope!

Oh, how they loved her!

And then, to the amazement of them all, something most wonderful happened….

Some people saw a light descend from Heaven. Others only heard the voice of their beloved Master, echoing from the sky.

Some saw the figure of Yeshua descending in the light, becoming brighter the closer it approached the Lady. Others felt only a strange warmth penetrating the gathering dusk— warmth which seemed to emanate from the woman who, standing transfixed, upon the rock, reached heavenward with greatest joy shining in her eyes.

The voice spoke to all present. They listened, stunned into silence.

"I HAVE COME TO CLAIM MY BRIDE," it declared, in tones as deep as oceans, as high as stars, and as soft as wind through the trees.

To those who did not understand, it might have seemed the echo of distant thunder on mountains to the north, or surf breaking upon the shore far to the south.

The apparition reached down to clasp the woman's outstretched hand, at last descending to stand beside her. At his touch, her body commenced to lighten, enfolded within his arms.

All eyes, to whom it was given to see, watched her figure become as luminous as his own. The two of them rose slowly into the light cascading down from above, light flowing from the hands of the other Mary, Queen of Heaven, stretched out in welcome.

Angels crowded around them, chanting music of the spheres... or could it have been birds singing sweetly to the spirit of evening?

The holy bride and bridegroom ascended higher, and higher, until a cloud hid them from sight.

And suddenly everything had vanished—the light, the warmth, the music.

Everything was as it had been before.

But no!

A crumpled figure had fallen, shrouded in her midnight blue cloak, to the foot of the meditation rock. The staff, the skull, the jar and book lay scattered on the ground around her.

"Mary!" shouted James, rushing to her side, lifting her into his arms. She was limp, inanimate, light as a feather.

"Mary!" he sobbed, cradling her lifeless form in sorrow. The cloak fell away from her face as he bent his head to kiss her.

The Magdalene was smiling.

* * * * *

POST SCRIPT

For years, if people had been present at the Magdalene's cave the day she died, they might have debated what happened in those few moments just before sunset. Around hearths in every village, stories of the miracle may have been repeated to children, and to the children's children. Each generation could have preserved the tale—sometimes changing in detail, but never in substance.

Before long, the story would likely have become a secret, passed down through underground societies— for the passage of seasons hastened epochs in which such knowledge was punished by torture or death.

And so it is, that from that time forward, many mysteries about Mary Magdalene have been kept hidden, by faithful believers, from Cathar to Templar, from that day to this one.

But no more.

There are no longer many secrets.

It has been promised that one day truth will begin to enlighten the world, banishing darkness.

That time is now.

The Magdalene is smiling.

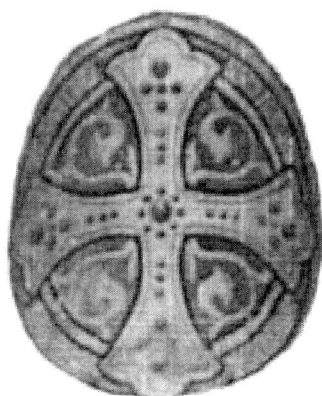

LIST OF RESOURCES

Baigent, Michael; Leigh, Richard & Lincoln, Henry; *Holy Blood, Holy Grail;* Dell Publishing, New York, 1983

Baigent, Michael; Leigh, Richard & Lincoln, Henry; *The Messianic Legacy;*Dell Publishing, New York, 1986

Begg, Ean; *The Cult of the Black Virgin;* Penguin Books, New York, 1996

Bolen, Jean Shinoda, M.D.; *Crossing to Avalon;*Harper, San Francisco, 1994

Braden, Gregg; *Awakening to Zero Point: The Collective Initiation;* Sacred Spaces/Ancient Wisdom, Questa, NM, 1994

Coughlan, Ronan; *The Encyclopaedia of Arthurian Legends;* Element Books, Rockport, MA, 1993

Culdian Movement of Mahara; *The book of Gwineva;* Culdian Movement of Mahara, Mahara, Tapu, New Zealand, 1981

Culdian Celestial Age Trust; *The Light of Truth: Wisdom from Rowena;*The Hope Trust, Thames, New Zealand, 1993

Fideler, David; *Jesus Christ, Sun of God: Ancient Cosmology & Early Christian Symbolism;* The Theosophical Publishing House, Wheaton, IL, 1993

Fuller, Simon Peter; *Rising Out of Chaos; The New Heaven & the New Earth;* Kima Global Publishers, Rondebosch, South Africa, 1996

244

Galland, China; *Longing for Darkness: Tara and the Black Madonna;*Penguin Books, USA, New York, 1991

Gardner, Laurence, The Chevalier Labhràn de St. Germain; *Bloodline of the Holy Grail: The Hidden Lineage of Jesus Revealed;* Element Books, Rockport, MA, 1996

Godwin, Malcolm; *The Holy Grail: Its Origins, Secrets & Meaning Revealed;* Viking Studio Books, Division of Penguin Books, New York, 1994

Goodrich, Norma Lorre; *The Holy Grail;* Harper Perennial, Division of Harper Collins Publisher, New York, 1992

Haskins, Susan; *Mary Magdalen: Myth and Metaphor;* Riverhead Books, The Berkley Publishing Group, New York, 1995

Hassnain, Professor Fida; *A Search for the Historical Jesus;* Gateway Books, Bath, U.K., 1994

The Holy Bible; Revised Standard Version, Second Edition, Reference Edition Thomas Nelson Inc., Nashville, TN, 1972

Howard-Gordon, Frances; *Glastonbury: Maker of Myths;* Gothic Image Publications, Glastonbury, Somerset, U.K., 1997

Kazmierski, Carl R.; *John the Baptist: Prophet and Evangelist;* The Liturgical Press, Collegeville, MN, 1996

Kerston, Holger & Gruber, Elmar R.; *The Jesus Conspiracy:The Turin Shroud & the Truth About the Resurrection;* Element Books, Rockport, MA, 1994

245

Kimball, Glenn & Stirland, David; *Hidden Politics of the Crucifixion;* Ancient Manuscripts Publishing, Salt Lake City, UT, 1998

Kinstler, Clysta; *The Moon Under Her Feet:The Story of Mari Magdalene in the Service of the Great Mother;* Harper San Francisco, Division of HarperCollins Publishers, 1989

Kokkinou, Sophia; *Greek Mythology;*Intercarta, Athens, Greece, 1989

Leeming, David & Page, Jake; Goddess: *Myths of the Female Divine;* Oxford University Press, New York, Oxford, 1994

Lockhart, Douglas; *Jesus, the Heretic: Freedom & Bondage in a Religious World;* Element Books, Rockport, MA, 1997

Loomis, Roger Sherman; *The Grail: From Celtic Myth to Christian Symbol;* Princeton University Press, Princeton, NJ, 1991

Maccoby, Hyam; *The Mythmaker: Paul and the Invention of Christianity;* Barnes & Noble Books, New York, 1998

Mann, Nicholas R.; *The Isle of Avalon: Sacred Mysteries of Arthur & Glastonbury Tor;* Llewellyn Publications, St. Paul, MN, 1996

Pagels, Elaine; *The Gnostic Gospels;*Vintage Books, Division of Random House, Inc., New York, 1979

Patton, Richard G.; *The Autobiography of Jesus of Nazareth and the Missing Years;* Amron Press, Vancouver, BC, 1997

Picknett, Lynn & Prince, Clive; *The Templar Revelation: Secret Guardians of the True Identity of Christ;* Touchstone, Simon & Schuster, New York, 1997

Ravenscroft, Trevor; *The Cup of Destiny: The Quest for the Grail;* Samuel Weiser, Inc., York Beach, ME, 1988

Sitchin, Zecharia; *The 12ᵗʰ Planet;* Bear & Company Publishing, Santa Fe, NM, 1991

Sora, Steven; *The Lost Treasure of the Knights Templar; Solving the Oak Island Mystery; Destiny Books, Rochester, VT, 1999*

Stanford, Ray; *Fatima Prophecy;* Ballantine Books, New York, 1987

Starbird, Margaret; *The Woman with the Alabaster Jar: Mary Magdalen and the Holy Grail;* Bear & Company Publishing, Santa Fe, NM, 1993

Starbird, Margaret; *The Goddess in the Gospels: Reclaiming the Sacred Feminine;* Bear & Company Publishing, Santa Fe, NM, 1998

Talbot, Michael; *The Holographic Universe;* Harper Perennial, Division of HarperCollins Publishers, New York, 1992

Thiering, Barbara; *Jesus the Man;* Corgi, Canada, Toronto, 1992

Thompson, Mary R., S.S.M.N.; *Mary of Magdala: Apostle and Leader;* Paulist Press, New York, 1995

Waters, Frank; *Masked Gods: Navaho and Pueblo Ceremonialism;* Ballentine Books, Inc., New York, 1973

Whitworth, Eugene E.; *Nine Faces of Christ: Quest of the True Initiate;* Great Western University Press, Renton, WA, 1986

Wood, David R.; *Genisis: The First Book of Revelations;* The Baton Press, Tunbridge Well, Kent, UK, 1985

Zimdars-Swartz, Sandra L; *Encountering Mary;* Avon Books, Division of the Hearst Corporation, New York, 1992

VIDEOTAPES

The Riddle of the Dead Sea Scrolls: Mysteries of the Bible Unravelled;
Discovery Enterprises Group, Bethesda, MD, 1992

The Templar Renaissance: The History of the Templar Movement;
Timon Films, in behalf of the Orcadian Trust; Roslin, Scotland;
Distributed by LL Productions, Bellevue, WA

WEBSITES

http://www.farjourneys.com/fornow.html
Judith Mann's website relating to the Cathars

http://www.themystica.com

On-line encyclopedia of religion and esoterica

http://www.le-minervois.com
Guide to Minervois area of Languedoc

http://www.le-guide.com
Guide to Provence

http://www.ariege.com
Guide to Ariège area of Languedoc

http://shekinah.elysiumgates.com/magdalene.html

http://www.magdalene.org

http://www.crystalinks.com/marymagdalene.html

http://www.halealexandria.org

Index

Britannia 40, 49, 92, 94

C

canonical 26
Capernaum 26
Carcassonne 46, 56, 73, 81, 111
Castelfranc 182
Cathar
  4, 36, 41, 46, 63, 64, 73, 74, 81, 86, 97, 101, 102, 111, 112, 113, 114, 115, 116,
  117, 118, 119, 127, 129, 135, 136, 137, 138, 139, 140, 141, 142, 144, 153, 154,
  155, 156, 167, 173, 182, 183, 231, 242, 248
Celt 42, 43, 50, 83, 246
Celtic 42, 43, 50, 83, 246
Chalice 40, 49
chalice 21, 41, 49, 121, 122, 215
Chambord 82
Chartres 225
Corinth 52
Cornwall 44
crop formation 3
Crucifixion 24, 246
crucifixion 3, 8, 183
Crusade 73, 81, 111, 183
Cybele 28, 32

D

DAGOBERT 83
Damascus 50, 52, 55
Davidic 26, 45
Dead Sea Scrolls 12, 135, 248
Demeter 28, 99
Demon 28
demon 10, 19, 29, 67
Devil 177
devil 28, 29, 75, 100
Diana 28, 35, 198
Dorade 174
duality 63, 75, 100
Dynastic 185
dynastic 185, 189, 192

251

E

Ean Begg 36
Egypt 17, 34, 35, 43, 63, 67, 71, 76, 101, 122, 138, 151, 218, 219
Elysian 44, 50
Essene 5, 12, 27, 64, 189, 190
Eucharia 26
Eve
        12, 20, 50, 54, 60, 66, 74, 76, 77, 99, 100, 108, 109, 110, 111, 112, 113, 118, 125,
        128, 135, 139, 141, 147, 164, 176, 177, 210, 212, 225, 240

G

Galilee 25
Gamaliel 53
Gaul 1, 12, 15, 29, 34, 40, 44, 49, 50, 52, 132, 134, 149, 188, 212
Gentile 35
Glastonbury 3, 44, 116, 225, 245, 246
Gnosis 36, 63
gnosis 102
Gnostic 26, 29, 36, 63, 64, 75, 101, 116, 246
Goddess
        28, 32, 33, 35, 36, 37, 43, 50, 66, 71, 97, 98, 100, 102, 103, 221, 246, 247
Gordes 200, 201, 203, 208, 218, 220, 224
Gospel 24, 25, 28, 29, 53, 246, 247
Gospel of Mary 29
Gospel of Philip 29
Gospel of Thomas 29
Grail 3, 4, 11, 21, 26, 28, 44, 68, 73, 76, 94, 98, 102, 148, 150,
        189, 215, 244, 245, 246, 247
Great Mother 219, 246
Greece 3, 35, 52, 53, 63, 99, 155, 229, 246
Greek 35, 101, 111, 246
Gypsy 34, 38, 193, 217, 218

H

Haskins, Susan 245
Hasmonaean 26
Heart to Peace Foundation 182
Hebrew 12, 26, 28, 35, 36, 45, 59, 66, 101, 192
Helena 4, 9, 17, 21, 23, 35, 91, 133, 134, 205, 210, 211, 216, 217
heresy 29, 81, 85

L

Languedoc
  3, 34, 41, 46, 55, 62, 63, 70, 81, 89, 111, 114, 124, 137, 183, 194, 249

Layerists 3
Lazarus 4, 9, 17, 91, 133, 134, 182, 193, 205, 206, 217, 218, 221
Leigh, Richard 244
Les Saintes-Maries-de-la-Mer 3, 17, 19, 20, 24, 30, 38
Lillith 32
Lincoln, Henry 244
Lombrives 154, 155
Luke 28, 53

M

Magdala 24, 25, 26, 28, 29, 30, 37, 74, 77, 86, 88, 89, 248
Magdalenian 46, 96, 158
Marriage 36, 184, 185
marriage
  1, 2, 7, 28, 87, 95, 98, 117, 123, 134, 181, 184, 185, 188, 189, 190, 191, 192, 193
Marseilles 3, 12, 13, 233
Martha
  4, 9, 17, 25, 52, 87, 182, 183, 188, 192, 194, 195, 196, 197, 198, 200, 201,
  202, 205, 206, 207, 213, 214, 221
Mary
  3, 4, 5, 8, 9, 10, 11, 12, 17, 19, 21, 24, 25, 26, 27, 28, 29, 30, 33, 34, 35, 37,
  38, 41, 43, 44, 45, 52, 55, 68, 75, 76, 77, 87, 94, 101, 102, 113, 133,
  135, 145, 174, 184, 185, 186, 192, 193, 194, 200, 209, 210, 211, 212,
  216, 217, 218, 219, 224, 225, 228, 229, 230, 231, 232, 233, 240, 241,
  242, 245, 247, 248
Mary Jacoba 4, 9, 17, 21, 145, 210, 211, 217
Mary Magdalene
  3, 4, 5, 8, 9, 10, 11, 17, 21, 24, 25, 26, 27, 30, 43, 44, 55, 68, 76, 102, 113, 135,
  174, 184, 185, 192, 193, 194, 200, 212, 225, 228, 229, 230, 231, 232, 233, 242
Matisse 18, 230
Maximim 3, 80, 91, 180, 181, 196, 200, 205, 213, 218, 221, 230, 233
Maximim-la-Sainte-Baume 3, 200
Menorah 28, 40
Messiah 54, 55
messiah 45, 191, 192
Minerve 102, 110, 111, 113, 114, 115, 124, 136

R

Ra 35, 46, 112, 123, 131, 137, 151, 246, 247
Raymond VI 112
Rennes-les-Bains 83, 84, 86, 95, 138
Revelations 219, 248
Rhedae 81
Roman
    9, 11, 26, 27, 29, 35, 36, 42, 43, 46, 50, 54, 55, 62, 63, 64, 70,
    71, 72, 73, 84, 87, 95, 101, 102, 110, 111, 112, 114, 117, 118,
    133, 136, 140, 150, 161, 176, 183, 233
Rome 27, 52, 81, 94, 102, 118

S

Saclas 108
Sadducee 1, 53, 54
Salome 26, 145, 217
Samael 108
Sarah 4, 9, 17, 34, 35, 36, 37, 38, 71, 91, 212, 215, 217, 218, 224
Satan 1, 28, 101, 177
Saul 10, 11, 12, 50, 52
serpent 109
Sidonius 205
Simon
    3, 29, 41, 81, 86, 113, 114, 115, 133, 134, 205, 217, 244, 247
Simon Magus 205, 217
Simon Peter 3, 29, 41, 244
SION 83, 235
Siran 41, 46, 52, 55, 56, 61, 70, 124, 182, 203
skull 4, 76, 77, 84, 85, 200, 214, 222, 229, 230, 231, 232, 239, 240
Song of Solomon 38, 193
Sophia 26, 37, 108, 109, 246
Spougla de Bouan 155
Starbird, Margaret 247

T

Tamar 7, 9, 91, 221, 235, 236, 237, 238
Tarascon 153, 156, 194, 198, 200, 201, 203
Tarasque 188
Tarsus 53
Templar Cross 89